🐾 *Bottom Line/Personal*
[One of] The Best Books on Self-Publishing.

🐾 John Kremer, *Book Marketing Update*
The best packaged book of all books on self-publishing. Nice looking. Easy to read.

🐾 Wanda Jewell, Southeast Booksellers Association
The message is that if you are going to self-publish, do it right, a message that bookstore owners know cannot be stated clearly enough.

🐾 Nigel Maxey, *Small Publisher* magazine
A fresh approach and design [that] is appealing inside and out....This volume will be a big help to many authors who are interested in publishing their own books.

🐾 Steve Carlson, *Big Books From Small Presses*
Congratulations on your success with *Smart Self-Publishing*. A lot of books come out on this topic, and yours seems to have joined the select few that are widely considered to be musts for the professional libraries of new publishers.

🐴 Betsy Lampé, reviewer, National Association of Independent Publishers

*Smart Self-Publishing* offers many insightful publishing stories, generous how-to-information, and the book, itself, is a great example of how a book should be put together. Publishing veterans Linda and Jim Salisbury provide their wisdom in another publishing bookshelf requisite.

🐴 Betty Wright, publisher, Rainbow Books

*Smart Self-Publishing* is a compendium of information. Well-organized and written for the layperson. Anyone thinking of publishing should read this book first.

🐴 Waldron A. McLellon, author, *Leather and Soul,* Butternut Press

It is an impressive book, beautiful on the outside, informative on the inside. It will be a valued addition to my library.

🐴 Dr. Robert Schissel, Ed.D., author, *The Art of Cooking Leftovers*

I read it cover to cover. As the sections on the many pitfalls that can (will) beset the novice author flashed past me, I swore I was reading my own biography. Where were you when I really needed you, [*before* I published my first book]?

# Smart Self-Publishing:

An author's guide to producing a marketable book

# Smart Self-Publishing:

An author's guide to producing a marketable book

Hot tips, sound advice, and publishing adventures from authors,
distributors, librarians, and book buyers

Linda and Jim Salisbury

With foreword by Joe Sabah

Second edition

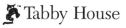 Tabby House

Manufactured in the United States of America
Library of Congress Catalog Card Number: 96-44431
ISBN: 1-881539-14-8
Illustrations: Christopher Grotke
Page design: Abigail Grotke
Cover design: Pearl and Associates
Setup and typography: Bob Lefebvre

**Library of Congress Cataloging-in-Publication Data**

Salisbury, Linda G. (Linda Grotke)
    Smart self-publishing : an author's guide to producing a
marketable book / Linda and Jim Salisbury : with foreword by Joe
Sabah. -- 2nd ed.
         p.   cm.
    "Hot tips, sound advice, and publishing adventures from authors,
distributors, librarians, and book buyers."
    Includes index.
    ISBN 1-881539-14-8 (pbk.)
    1. Self-publishing --United States.   I. Salisbury, Jim, 1936–
II. Title.
Z285.5.S25   1997
070.5'93--dc21
                                          96-44431
                                           CIP

 Tabby House
4429 Shady Lane
Charlotte Harbor, Florida 33980
(941) 629-7646, fax (941) 629-4270
E-mail: Publisher@TabbyHouse.com
Web site: http://www.tabbyhouse.com/publish/

To kith, kin, and smart self-publishing authors.

# Contents

# Foreword

IT's EASY TO WRITE A BOOK. It's easy to publish a book. The hard part? Doing it right.

As the author of three books and co-owner of a small publishing house in Denver, Colorado, I speak from experience when I say that books must be properly produced. I also know that if a self-publishing author develops a marketing strategy and makes good use of available free publicity, such as becoming a guest on radio talk shows, the book can be sold profitably.

*Smart Self-Publishing*, by Linda and Jim Salisbury, tells the stories of successful self-publishers and provides numerous tips that will help you create a product that will sell. The Salisburys and I have seen many examples of books that were produced professionally and filled a market niche, and also, unfortunately, many that were doomed to failure because the author did not understand how to do a book right. When authors contact me about my second book, *How to Get on Radio Talk Shows All Across America Without Leaving Your Home or Office,* they often send copies of their books. I wish you could browse my bookshelves as you read this foreword. Most of the books are top quality—books that anyone would be proud to have their name on. Unfortunately, quite a few definitely need help—let me change that to "needed help"—*before* they went to press.

How can we tell? One way is to look at the spines. You'd think that everyone would know that the spine should always read from the top to the bottom. That's the right way. But on my shelf I find five books where the printing started at the bottom, making it not only awkward but uncomfortable to read the title. This shows that the book is the work of an amateur. You certainly want your book to look like the books produced by mainstream publishing houses!

Now let's look at the covers. Why, oh why, do some self-publishers think that the more colors they use, the better? The obviously homemade books stand out on my shelves because of covers that do not look like those of mainstream publishing houses.

These books are doomed as unprofessional products, and we haven't even opened them yet! Inside we find typos, no table of contents, no index, no Library of Congress Catalog Card Number, no ISBN. No title or half-title page, poor margins, and hard-to-read type. Each of these omissions not only distracts but marks the book as "the product of an amateur." Will this affect sales? You bet!

Thank goodness help is here. Linda and Jim Salisbury have created a recipe for doing it right—the first time. Their recipe book, *Smart Self-Publishing*, now in the second, even more helpful edition, walks you step-by-step through the details of book publishing from production to promoting and selling your book.

If I could pass one law, it would read: "Thou shalt not even think about publishing your own book until you've read and put to use all the information in *Smart Self-Publishing*."

This valuable book will not only save you a bundle of money—if you follow the recipe, and do it right—but it can help you make a bundle of money when you are ready to sell your books.

JOE SABAH
Denver, Colorado

# Preface

*. . . It doesn't have to be a dark and stormy night!*

MOST OF US WRITERS can relate to Charles Schulz's Snoopy, a beloved member of the syndicated cartoon strip, "Peanuts." Through the years the family beagle struggles with his novel from atop his doghouse, never getting beyond the first few sentences. But what will Snoopy do with the manuscript when he finally reaches the conclusion? Will he try to find an agent? Perhaps Lucy? Or will he make a copy of his manuscript to send to Random House or Simon & Schuster? Snoopy has name recognition, which could help him get a paw in the door, but generally it's difficult, if not impossible, for unknown authors to sell the rights to their books—especially novels or poetry—to a major publishing house.

To find out just how hard it is to have good material even read at big publishing houses, *The Weekly*, an Orlando magazine, tried an experiment. Reporter David Wilkening was fed up with reading what he considered to be bad books put out by major publishers. He wondered if any of the literary giants of the past could be published today. To test his idea, his magazine submitted Marjorie Kinnan Rawlings' Pulitzer Prize-winning novel, *The Yearling*, under a phony title, to twenty-two publishers. Most didn't even read it. All but one—a Florida publisher who recognized the book—either rejected or ignored it.

An Associated Press article[1] describing Wilkening's experiment concluded that "... publishers and authors agree that things have changed since 1938 [when *The Yearling* was originally published]."

Elizabeth Silverthorne, Rawlings' biographer, was quoted by the Associated Press as saying, "Now it is rare for a newcomer's book to be snapped up unless it has the backing of a literary agent or a famous author. In the old days, the publishers were more independent, and they could look into quality. Now, they're concerned only with how much a book will sell."

Writers should not be discouraged by present publishing conditions nor should they spend their lives waiting "to be discovered." Snoopy does not want to end up outside his dog house on a dark and stormy night with a pile of rejection slips and nothing to show for his dreams. Neither do you! If you believe in your work, you should thoroughly investigate the ways to beat the system and get your book published.

One of these options is self-publishing.

What is self-publishing? Simply put, it is you taking control of your own publishing destiny by doing your book yourself. That means putting your money into the project, and then becoming actively involved in the production of the book and in its marketing and distribution. It also means personally reaping the profits. Snoopy may have heard that a number of nationally selling books were first self-published by their authors. But our literary beagle has also been warned by well-meaning friends about getting involved with vanity or subsidy presses: "They can be a rip-off, and you might not get much satisfaction or many copies of your book for your money." A few first-time authors have created professional products on their own, but they are the fortunate, but perhaps accidental exceptions because beginners are usually unaware of the details of publishing. Most of the others are finding that it is worth investigating contracting the services of a quality book packager.

This alternative meets the need to make the book a professional product. After all, like most writers, Snoopy has put a lot of time and work into it. He doesn't want his book to look homemade.

Sound like a familiar story? Fortunately, thanks to professional book packagers or producers, there can be a happy ending.

A few rights-buying publishers, some independent publishers, some printers and even some one-title author/publishers offer packaging services as a sideline to their businesses. Wise consumers will explore various options carefully, and will ask for references. The end result must be professional and marketable so that you can recoup your investment and even make a profit.

That's what this book is about. It is to give courage and direction to prospective self-publishers. It is written by self-publishers who eventually became publishers and book packagers for other authors. It contains a wealth of information about publishing based on advice given to us by book distributors, buyers, publishers, marketers, editors, other authors and on our actual experiences. Please note that some of the authors mentioned in the book are not self-published, but we believe their experiences are relevant to any discussion of publishing.

We've tried to make this book honest, informative, and easy to use. Throughout the text we have flagged useful tips with the pencil graphic, and true stories and publishing adventures with the typewriter symbol.

This book can be used as a guide to self-publishing by those who want to attempt it on their own, or by those who seek to have someone else create a book for them from their manuscript. It is intended to help you get started, make you aware of those things a book needs to be professional, and point you in the right direction for selling your book. It is not meant to be an encyclopedia, nor does it pretend to have all the answers. At times it shamelessly promotes our own business—professional book packaging. We wouldn't be following our own advice if we didn't try to sell our product.

As independent publishers and book packagers, our philosophy of self-publishing is rather simple: If you, the author, do not have enough faith in your book to consider investing in it yourself, why should you think publishing houses will put their money into it? If you feel your book is worth creating, and you can arrange the finances, do it—but do it right!

LINDA AND JIM SALISBURY

# Acknowledgments

We appreciate the suggestions and comments of the many individuals who are quoted by permission in this book. Some are authors for whom we have packaged books; many others are not.

We are grateful to the self-publishing authors, and others who have read various drafts both editions of *Smart Self-Publishing* and shared their thoughts, experiences, and red-proofing pens. Among them: Pam Gastineau, Jim Robertson, Howard Irons, Nancy Wettlaufer, Dianne Warren, Maria Fineout and Sharon Rendell. And we appreciate the encouragement of those who buy and distribute books, and the support we have gotten from our fellow publishers. Most of all, we have enjoyed hearing from the many people around the country who found our first edition helpful as they contemplated or worked on their book projects.

We are especially thankful for the talents of Christopher Grotke, who created the graphics, Abigail Grotke for the page-design concept, Bob Lefebvre for his skill in layout and typesetting, and Chris Pearl for his brilliant cover design.

# 1 Ways to get published

*I'm not clear whether self-publishing is the way to go. Somehow I have this feeling that by going that route, I am admitting that my efforts are not good enough for publication.*—Author still looking for a publisher to buy her manuscript—*after six years!*

ONCE UPON A TIME, as the story in the introduction goes, the publishing world was quite different from what it is today. People wrote books—poetry, essays, and novels. They sent their manuscripts off to publishing houses in big cities and agents or editors often chased them down with a contract. Advances were paid and sometimes royalties followed. Unknown authors—if they were any good— had a chance. The publishing industry has changed dramatically, though, and yesterday's publishing success story is usually today's fairy tale.

This does not mean that writers today won't be able to find outlets for their books. Certainly some will be purchased, but most will not. This book is written for the latter group. Their success story may well be found in self-publish-ing—especially if the actual work of publishing is done properly by the author, possibly using the services of a professional book packager.

Many writers raised on the "fairy tale" need further convincing. They have been charmed by the old publishing mystique: If a publisher doesn't buy my book, it isn't any good. This is a self-defeating spell that keeps those writers from the satisfaction of having their manuscripts turned into books. It is, in fact, the ulti-mate vanity of publishing!

While the authors who still believe in this myth are living in fantasy land, many other authors are successfully self-publishing.

Why are writers driven to find someone else to buy rights to their book in order to have their work validated? Compare this way of thinking with that of any other independent creative group: artists, musicians, and photographers. Most independent artists purchase their own supplies, rent studio space, and cooperatively show their work in galleries. They are looking for sales and good reviews, yes. But they paint, or play music, and invest in their work regardless of grants or patronage. Why should books and literature be different from paintings or sculpture?

The doers have their book in hand and, if the book is produced properly, no one is able to tell the difference between an author/publisher-produced book and one done by a major publishing house. *Publishers Weekly*[2] repeatedly underscores the problems in the present publishing market at the big houses. Nora Rawlinson, editor-in-chief, writes: "Publishing has always had to deal with the uncomfortable tension between art and commerce and has often had to leave to posterity—in the form of backlist sales [those books which have old copyright dates and are relegated to the back section of a sales catalog]—the final choice on what works over the long haul."

She continues: "It has been a common complaint among booksellers for years that there are simply too many books, which means that a book's shelf life continually shrinks. This has led to discussion within the industry about the need to publish fewer titles, so that each book receives the attention it requires to find its audience."

There are several reasons for the shift from the old days of publishing to the new, but the overriding cause is money. Publishing is big business and there is an increasing emphasis on viewing books as *products,* in competition with other products, rather than as literature for literature's sake. It's hard for writers to accept the fact that their book is a product on which publishing houses must be able to make a return on their investment. But that is the situation and you should want the same results with your product—your book. If you don't, then perhaps you should consider printing only enough copies to give away to your family and friends.

It takes money to produce the product. It takes money to advertise the product—lots of money on the national level, perhaps hundreds of thousands of dollars per title. Even writers with nationally known names need the boost of marketing hype. The cover of the August 5, 1996 issue of *Publishers Weekly* trumpets:

"KING of the SEASON Stephen King roars into Fall with two new titles backed by a multimillion-dollar marketing campaign."

It is very difficult for small press to compete with this kind of blitz.

Experienced book promoters who arrange author tours and television interviews tell us it is difficult, if not impossible, to work for an author or publisher with a promotion budget less than $5,000.

The small publishers refer to the major national publishers as "The Big Guys." The large publishing houses, many owned by conglomerates (Bigger Guys), want a fast return on their investment and so they look for hot topics or hot authors. They are unwilling to invest in risky projects. Frankly, it doesn't matter how good the author's material is. It doesn't matter that friends and acquaintances are truly sincere when they tell writers that they think they should be published. If the material does not fit into a publishing house's marketing line, they will not buy it. Realistically, most unknown writers do not fit into the needs of the "Big Guys."

Competition is stiff. The reading market is increasingly limited as people use electronic technology for information and recreation.

Writers become discouraged when they find that New York City

A California writer sold his book, which dealt with how to make TV commercials, to a major publisher a few years ago. He received a $5,000 advance, but he is frustrated because there is, so far, no book.

Someone at the publishing house decided against taking the book beyond the acquisition stage. Perhaps the topic was deemed no longer hot; perhaps another publisher put out a similar book. All the author knows is that he worked hard, sold his rights, and probably will never see his book in print—unless he gets his rights back and self-publishes. He is not alone in this experience.

publishers aren't interested in reading, let alone buying, material by unknown writers, especially fiction and poetry which is, unfortunately, what most first-time authors have been busy writing.

A front-page article in the April 28, 1996 edition of the *New York Times* points to the growing success of self-publishers, thanks to desktop publishing. In the last

 There is a terrific market for regional books. People visiting or living in a particular area will buy books about it. Think of tailoring your material to a geographic region in order to capture that market. (See Chapter 3.)

ten years, the "number of new small publishers has increased by more than 200 percent, to a record 5,514 last year." Reporter Doreen Carvajal notes that those figures include just those new publishers who applied for bar codes [ISBN registry] through the Reed Refer-

 Ann Rust, a writer of Florida historical fiction, sent out a dozen queries, but while waiting for responses began looking into self-publishing. She then took control. Her husband said he would serve as editor, and together they started their own publishing house, Amaro Books, which has published five of her novels.

Ann works hard to sell her books. Hardly a week goes by that she is not doing a booksigning or appearing on local talk shows as part of her marketing campaign. Her books are in libraries and bookstores throughout the region and are thoroughly enjoyed by readers who like a fast-paced, fun-read while being educated about early Florida life. The profits from Ann's early successes fund her new projects and reprints.

ence Company [parent company of R.R. Bowker]. Carvajal adds that "Self-publishers also doubled their submissions in the last year and a half to Barnes & Noble, the nation's largest bookstore chain."

That's tough competition, especially for writers without a publishing record.

Even when a publisher purchases material there is still no guarantee that the book will be produced—even if the author has received an advance.

## Maintaining control

Many authors self-publish because they want to maintain total control over their product or because they want to maximize their profits. Control can be an important issue, although we certainly recommend listening to editing and packaging experts, especially if you want a professional product.

Jim Robertson self-published a national award-winning book on the history of public television. Robertson, who used a book packaging service, notes that editing control is very important. He had originally submitted his manuscript to a publishing company that had very different views on what was happening in public television programming. "I think editors can easily pervert the author's intended meaning if they are not careful," he said. "Author involvement can keep that from happening."

Control means that you have input in decisions regarding the text, cover, and title. Control means that the book will actually be produced, rather than be left on the shelf in the office of a rights-buying publisher. Control means that a self-publishing author will make the marketing decisions. A celebrity who self-publishes an autobiography can decide how and when to make personal appearances, because it is his or her money backing the book. There is no pressure from rights-buying publishers to go on a media tour to help them sell the book in which they have invested.

## Self-publishing is gaining respect

Self-published books, if they are professionally produced, can demonstrate their market appeal and sometimes can be sold to book clubs or to rights-buying publishers after the first printing. Self-publishing gets your book into the bookstores and in the marketplace where it can prove itself. Agents and representatives of the Big Guys are watching for intriguing self-published books. They can be impressed by entrepreneurial spirit and an author's willingness to absorb risk and take the profits of the project.

Consider the recent success of *The Christmas Box*, by Richard Paul Evans. According to an article by Lawrence Van Gelder in the *New York Times*[3], Evans wrote the story in 1992 for his family and had twenty copies printed by a local printer. By February 1993, people were asking for it in bookstores. He then sent the book to regional publishers was rejected, and decided to publish the story himself. By December 1994, the book was in the No. 2 position on the newspaper's paperback best-seller list and sales were approaching 400,000 copies.

Of course not every self-published book will have such a fortunate public reception and national success. Evans obviously had a unique Christmas story that appealed to readers—and he was willing to invest in his product.

Or consider the story of Aliske Webb's book, *Twelve Golden Threads: Lessons for Successful Living from Grama's Quilt*. According to *Publishers Weekly*[4], Webb had been rejected by all one hundred fifty publishers that she had submitted the book to. She and her husband decided to self-publish and sold the initial press run of 3,000 copies at quilt shows. She hit a market niche and sold 25,000 copies in less than three years. When the book was pur-

 Denny Moore and his wife, Velda, set sail one day from Chesapeake Bay and ended up traveling around the world. Moore wrote and self-published their adventures in *Gentlemen Never Sail to Weather* (Prospector Press). His book was chosen by the Book-of-the-Month Club as an alternate selection. He has already published a second edition and a second book, *Alaska's Lost Frontier,* a contemporary history about life in the days of homesteads, dog teams, and sailboat fisheries. He has found a market for unusual travel stories and boating stories, and works diligently to get them sold.

chased by HarperCollins, the initial printing was 62,000 copies.

Other self-publishers (also referred to in the publishing world as author/publishers or self-publishing authors) have watched their books receive national attention after first demonstrating salability in smaller markets.

Two other self-published books which have had enough success to gain national attention and sale to a larger publishing house are Beth Fowler's, *Could You Love Me Like My Dog?*, and *Could You Love Me Like My Cat?* According to *Publishers Weekly*[5], Fowler's books were successful in her home state, Texas, largely through her own promotional efforts (including selling books out of her pickup truck at rodeos). Her success caught the attention of Simon & Schuster. Her books have been republished under that imprint and are selling well.

The key to successful self-publishing is to make quality the top priority. Quality should guide all decisions in the production of the book. There is no reason that a self-published book should look homemade unless the self-publisher creates it that way through lack of knowledge or by misplaced thrift. A book packager can provide the type of direction that is needed to guide the publishing process so that doesn't happen.

Writers who want to see if their manuscript can be sold to a rights-buying publisher should send queries to those publishers who deal in the kind of book they have written. In other words, send mysteries to publishers who primarily publish mysteries rather than sending copies to every publishing house listed in *Writer's Market*. Research the small presses to see which ones have specialties that might dovetail with your material. The easiest way to do this is to go to a bookstore or library and make a list of publishers of the type of material you have written. Or read trade magazines such as *Publishers Weekly* or newsletters from a publishers' association such as the National Association of Independent Publishers. (See Appendix B.) By so doing, you will be able to compile data about niche publishers (such as science fiction, romance, and westerns) that specialize in specific topics.

In some instances you can find an agent who will do the legwork to help find a publisher who will purchase your manuscript. Increasingly, though, agents are requiring an up-front fee for their efforts rather than a fee contingent upon sale of your book. Some agents handle only certain types of books, such as action and adventure, while others specialize in selling subsidiary rights for any already-published author to magazines, other publishers, large-print editions, or foreign rights.

### Vanity press

Through the years, vanity press has given self-publishing a negative image. Vanity press implies that authors are self-publishing for egotistical reasons—out of vanity—and maybe sometimes they are. That is not necessarily bad, if the project is done well.

Unfortunately, a number of authors who have been rejected for various reasons by the Big Guys subsequently have been seduced and ripped off by a vanity press. The bottom line is that the author usually pays more—sometimes as much as triple what it would have cost to produce the book themselves using the services of a quality book packager. And, usually the author relinquishes the rights to their work, sometimes for two years while the publisher "markets" the book, sometimes forever.

The author might receive thirty, fifty, or perhaps even one hundred copies of the book as part of the contract, and then must purchase additional copies from the vanity press "publisher." The rest of the books vanish—if they were ever printed at all. They are rarely sold in bookstores, except in remainder bins, or even widely marketed. The vanity press may even use the author-paid-for copies as sample books to attract more potential clients. We have had authors tell us, with some embarrassment, that they have paid $18,000 or $20,000 to have their book published by a vanity press, and have ended up with only one hundred or fewer copies for their own use. It is hard to recoup your investment if you have only one hundred copies to sell on your own—which in effect cost two hundred dollars each—and the "publisher" is not really marketing the rest of the copies.

## Subsidy press

Simply put, subsidy means that the author pays to publish. There is a distinct difference between paying to produce through packaging, or through the typical "subsidy press" (a variation on the theme of vanity). When you work with a packager you will usually have your own imprint and ISBN. All the

 Caveat emptor! Be a smart consumer. Check with your local bookstores and libraries. Ask if they receive a catalog from these subsidy presses and if they order from them. Find out if the books published by subsidy presses are properly credentialed. (See Chapter 4.) for bookstore sales. Know what marketing you will actually get for the price.

rights to the book will be yours. Usually a subsidy press will apply its ISBN to your work. Sometimes it will also claim the copyright.

It is essential for anyone considering using a vanity or subsidy press, a book packager or printer to be a careful consumer and not be mislead by promises. We have talked to authors whose egos are being stroked by the clever marketing approaches. A subsidy press often will rave over the author's work, and tell the author that the publisher will contribute *half the production and the marketing costs* if the author will contribute the other half. Oddly enough, the author who is a good consumer and does some shopping around probably will discover that the amount he or she is expected to contribute is actually more than what it would cost to have the book packaged correctly. Again, the author, who has paid for an entire press run, actually receives only a fraction of the alleged press run and must purchase additional copies from the subsidy publisher.

Sometimes the author will be promised a royalty based on a percentage after a certain number of copies are sold. Rarely does that occur. The promised marketing is usually an "extra," and can be quite pricey. The subsidy press usually offers to list the book in its catalog or to send out some press releases for fliers. These catalogs typically do not generate many, if any, sales, and the author could easily do his or her own press release.

There are many variations of these themes, but the essence— that the author pays a lot and doesn't get much in return—is always the same.

In fairness, anyone thoroughly reading the promotional material for most vanity and subsidy presses will see that these companies are careful to offer disclaimers for the sales potential of a book, and some specify marketing "opportunities" at extra cost. They are also forthright about the fact that you are responsible for subsidizing the project, and in return will receive 40 percent of the retail price as compensation, *if* any copies of the book are sold. Several brochures we have examined from subsidy presses make it clear that an unknown author is a hard sell and that the press' marketing efforts are limited to press releases and catalogs. This information is couched between enthusiastic testimonials that imply that subsidy presses successfully sell books. One such press says that it promotes the sale of its books by telephone, correspondence, direct mail, catalogs, and by the authors, themselves.

To underscore the pertinent points authors should compare when getting bids on estimates from various types of presses: the number of actual copies to be received; the quality of the product and success of whatever marketing is part of the promise (Ask for samples and references, then contact the other authors.); and how much control does the author have in the project.

## Printers are not publishers

So, why not just take your book to a printer? Because, for one thing, printers are *not* publishers. Printing is just one part of the publishing process. Printers usually do not edit your work for grammar and style. And, they do not issue the credentials your book needs to be accepted in the marketplace. Only publishers can do that. Beyond that, most printers print the copy they are given just as it is given to them. If your camera-ready is of

We know of a bookstore owner who was so convinced that a local author would produce a national best-seller that he helped finance the book. Unfortunately the bookseller provided only money, not expertise, and the production of the book was a disaster. The amateurish cover was the least of its problems. The text was not well edited and the book was not typeset. During the printing process, ink from the plates got on the rollers and pages were superimposed. Instead of having a salable product, the store owner ended up hiding the cartons of books in his storage room. This may be an extreme case of bad production, but it certainly is a caution for you to see that your product is produced properly.

poor quality, is smudged, or if the pages are not aligned, or if you have typed your book rather than had it typeset, that is how the book will be printed. Printers may not know that you have your book title upside down on the spine or that you should have a printed back cover.

Printers also are usually not aware of book style. They may be able to typeset your pages, but often they are out of their element when it comes to creating a proper book. We have seen many examples of books printed and bound by printers, and most of them lack the professional look. Does that make a difference? You bet! That is, if you want to be able to sell your book rather than just give it away to relatives and friends. A homemade or poor-quality appearance can doom even the finest piece of writing. Unless a manuscript needs extensive editing or rewriting, much of the cost of producing a book is in the cover design, page formatting, typesetting, and the printing and binding. It is important to produce your book professionally, even if it costs more.

Ron Watson, a book buyer at Ingram Books, one of the nation's largest wholesalers, told the members of the Florida Publishers Association that Ingram will not handle a book that doesn't have a proper cover and credentials, including a bar code. These issues are of no concern to the average printer.

### Book packaging

That brings us to book packaging or book producing. A book packager has the expertise of a publisher but works for you rather than buying or taking the rights to your book. Except under certain conditions, your packager will assist you in obtaining the credentials for your book in the name of your own publishing imprint.

Some companies specialize in book packaging. A few rights-buying publishers, some independent publishers, some printers and even some one-title author/publishers, distributors and others advertise packaging services as a sideline to their business. As a good consumer, you need to explore your options. Ask for samples and references and discuss the range of services that are available to you. Costs will vary tremendously based on what your book needs, such as editing or indexing, and special features you may choose, such as the type of cover or paper stock. You may get a cheaper bid from a "cookie-cutter" packager than from someone who tailors an estimate to your needs.

A book packager acts as your contractor to build your book. The copyright is yours. The book will be fully credentialed in your name and will be carefully designed. You will be involved in decisions about the cover, the design, the paper stock, the editing, the size of the press run, and the retail price. And most important, you will receive *all the copies called for in your contract*—all of them! You are the one risking the money, so you should be the person to receive and control the product. And, if you are willing to do the work to market and sell your book, you will reap the ultimate profit.

**Financing your book**

Some self-publishers have personal resources to invest in their product; others find financial backers. The backer may be a relative or friend, or, if it is a biography, even the person who is the subject of the book; or the money may come in the form of a grant from an organization or foundation. Con-sider approaching an outside party to help with the financing for a share of the profits. For example, if you have written about caring for a child who has suffered a head injury, or if you have an unusual cancer treatment story, research or social organizations might help offset your costs. Having their name on the book also may help increase your sales.

Mull over these words of advice from Betsy Lampé, marketing director at Rainbow Books in Highland City, Florida, and executive director of the National Association of Independent Publishers: "There is only one caveat to self-publishing: Don't hock the house or the kids' college fund. Publishing is always risky at best (something even the New York publishers understand), and a potential self-publisher should never embark on a project if its failure portends financial disaster for the author or for the author's family."

# 2 How book packaging can work for you

*Harried authors may find it worthwhile to farm out production to a pro. . . . Such consultants [packagers] are different from vanity publishers. Book consultants work for a pre-set fee; profits are yours.*
— U.S. News & World Report[6]

YOUR INITIAL CONTACT with a book packager, either by phone, mail, personal meeting or even on the Internet, should allow you to get an idea of the company's philosophy and range of services, possible costs, and estimated production time. You should ask for a list of references as well as a list of books that the packager has produced. Ask for a production sample of the company's work. After you have reviewed the information, make an appointment to discuss your project in detail. Ideally this should be a personal meeting, but if that is impossible, prepare a list of questions and use the telephone.

While you probably want to know what your book will cost to produce, be careful about trying to pin the packager down to a de-tailed figure at this stage. There is so much variation in the costs of book production that it is difficult to generalize estimates. It's like going to a real estate agent and saying, "Tell me what a house costs." There are many variables in houses and books that determine the range of prices.

Your packager should ask for detailed information about your material and may request sample pages to determine how much editing or rewriting may be in-volved. You should have general discussions about the possible appearance of the book: the best size, type of cover, the kind of paper, possible fonts (including appropriate size), whether to use photographs or art, color or black and white, and other details. You should also discuss your thoughts about the size of the press run and the retail price of the book (if it is to be sold through retail outlets).

Once all the details are factored in, the company should be able to give you an estimate tailored to your specific book—a figure that obviously will change if you decide to add or remove pages, change the number of photographs, the size of the book or the press run.

Some packagers will give you a flat figure for producing your book based on a set cost per page for one thousand, two thousand or more copies. Typically the fee will cover only typesetting, printing and binding plus a "cookie-cutter" cover design. It may or may not include credentialing. This arrangement may work to some authors' advantage and not to others, depending on the condition of the manuscript and the amount of work involved. Books need varying amounts of developing. Usually the flat, per-page fee includes using computer spellcheck, but won't include the line editing or rewriting that many manuscripts need, especially those written by first-time authors. Find out what you will get for a flat fee.

A good packager will not just take your manuscript and say, "How nice," and print it. Good packaging includes editorial and design counseling as well as book production. The availability of good editing is one of the major services that may separate the professional packagers from the vanity and subsidy presses.

Editing is probably one of the most important aspects of publishing and probably one of the most sensitive to deal with. Some authors are married to their prose, no matter how much work it needs. Others believe that their book is "camera ready" because they have had a friend or family member "edit it."

A first-class book packager should do the same job that a rights-buying publisher would do—namely, produce a quality product for the marketplace.

## Good editing

Few writers want to admit when they first seek a publisher or packager that they need help with the editing or organizing of their book. Writers can be very sensitive people. Nobody likes to see the red pencil used on his or her copy, but good editing is often essential to the book's success.

In early 1993 we met Dr. Howard Irons, a retired physician, who had written a book about his wife, Rae, a registered nurse who had been diagnosed two years earlier with glioblastoma multiforme—a particularly virulent form of brain cancer. They were told that there was no effective treatment available for her condition. After resigning themselves to Rae's medically hopeless situation, the couple learned of a treatment called Boron Neutron Capture Therapy (BNCT), which was available in Japan. Skeptical, but without other options, Howard and Rae traveled to Japan for the treatment. Not only was BNCT successful for Rae, but the Irons learned about how other lives (including those of other Americans) had been saved through BNCT.

As Rae resumed an active life the couple became involved in a crusade to make the treatment available in the United States. They twice testified before congressional subcommittees, and wrote many letters to government officials and to newspapers. Dr. Irons was doing more than writing letters. In harmony with his medical training, he had kept detailed notes on Rae's initial diagnosis, first surgery in the United States, and subsequent treatment in Japan. These notes and his diary became the basis for the book he initially didn't know he was writing. Eventually he ended up with several hundred pages of typewritten narrative. Because of the interest in the BNCT experience, people kept asking for copies and suggested that it should be made into a book. Dr. Irons sent copies of his manuscript to several publishers. All returned it for a variety of reasons. One said that it would take too much editing and rewriting. Another had just published a medical book and wasn't interested in something similar so soon.

There was little question that the manuscript needed both surgery and treatment. Fortunately, the Irons (and we share their story with permission) knew they needed assistance and were willing to accept editorial direction. The end product is barely recognizable to friends and colleagues who saw early versions, but is receiving rave reviews from them and from total strangers for its content, readability, scientific information, human interest, and emotion.

The Irons also understood the need for a dramatic cover, and followed advice about endorsements for the back cover. As a result of the book's "package," a national distributor held the deadline on its 1994 spring catalog to include *Rae of Hope* as its first selection.

A packager who tells you that your work needs editing is like your best friend who tells you that your breath is bad. You might not like the message, but the advice could save the day. Skilled editors can make your product shine. We cannot say enough good about the value of the constructive editing process.

From personal experience, we well know the difference between good, constructive editing that polishes, clarifies, organizes, and improves a writer's work, and bad editing. Bad editing is nothing more than shuffling words and rewriting without regard to the author's style. It is often the result of someone else's ego and desire to impose his or her own style on the author's work. Nothing is worse than bad editing. Conversely, nothing is better for your manuscript than good editing.

Other writers may have been told how wonderful their material was by people who didn't want to hurt the writer's feelings or by people who didn't know the reality of the market. Good editors will give advice and make recommendations to improve your book. But don't hesitate to ask questions, challenge changes, or to tell editors why you feel a paragraph or word is important.

Good editing is more than working on sentence structure while maintaining the author's style. It will also include suggestions for expanding sections, strengthening characters, making cuts, or rewriting for clarification.

A book packager or editor should be addressing very basic marketing questions. Who is your reader? If the answer is, "The average person.", then you should not be writing in the language of an academician or physician. Your vocabulary, examples and explanations must be geared to your specific audience. A good editor should point you in the right direction. How much time does your reader have to spend on your book? If the intended audience is very busy, you should shorten sections to keep material focused and sparkling to hold interest.

The more you do to provide "clean copy" to the editor, the easier it will be for your book packager or publisher, and the easier it will be on your wallet. By clean copy we mean having spelling grammar, and punctuation as correct as possible and with no messy hand-written changes in the margins or between the lines.

Sometimes an editor may suggest reorganizing the entire book. Be willing to listen to and consider all ideas that will help sell and market your book.

There are also free-lance "book doctors" who advertise their availability to authors in need of manuscript surgery. If you are considering contracting for editing services prior to dealing with a book packager, be a careful consumer. Over the years we have received many manuscripts that were supposed to have been "edited" by so-called professionals or by friends of the author, that needed to be redone. The work did not adhere to book style or even acceptable grammar. There were still gaps in the flow and obvious changes in writing style where the editors had inserted material.

 One author we know, to show respect for church hierarchy, insisted on capitalizing all religious titles in his text: the Bishop, the Priest, the Pope. Wrong! Both stylebooks are specific on this issue. If you are using a title before a person's name, capitalize it: Bishop Scotto, Pope Paul. If the person's title follows the name, it is lower case. Paul Jones, bishop. When used alone, these titles are not capitalized either. For instance, "The priest is coming to dinner."

Check references and costs, and ask for before and after samples of their work. If possible, negotiate fixed prices rather than an hourly rate. If you are dealing separately with editors and book doctors on an hourly basis, and are not careful, the cost of editing could end up being more than the price of printing and binding your book.

One of the benefits of being a self-publisher and working with a book packager is that since you are paying for the production of the book, you are the boss and as such, you have the right to reject advice if you feel the book doesn't benefit from the changes. Even so, we strongly suggest that you keep an open mind. Book packagers and their editors will be looking at the editing job not just sentence by sentence, but to see how your material can be made into a book that flows and has logical continuity. Sometimes your editor will send you back to the keyboard to reorganize or rework a section; sometimes to the dictionary, a stylebook, the library or even back to sources to check facts and provide additional documentation.

## Book "style"

A good book packager will require that its editors and proof readers check for "style." What is style? Simply stated, style standardizes spellings, abbreviations, and hyphenation. Style dictates when to use numerals for numbers or when to spell them out, when to italicize titles and when to put them in quotation marks, and when to capitalize words. Use standard stylebooks, such as *The Chicago Manual of Style*, published by the University of Chicago Press, in conjunction with *The Associated Press Stylebook,* and a quality dictionary. The use of stylebooks provides the industry with standards and your use of one will lend professionalism to your text. Sometimes the suggested style changes may go against your grain, but if you want your book to be mainstream, then consistency and conformity to book style is important.

For example, schools teach that all titles should be underlined or within quotation marks, but titles are not underlined in book style. They are either in italics (books) or within quotation marks (articles). Titles of poems, songs, television shows, movies, newspapers and magazines, dramatic works have their own rules. You will want to check *The Chicago Manual of Style* for proper style basics.

If you find inconsistencies you will have to establish your own style. For example, a number of years ago when we were working on a book about public television, our editors discovered that "noncommercial" was also correctly

Don't guess. Check all compound words, all names, all foreign words, and all abbreviations with the stylebooks and dictionaries.

written "noncommercial." We decided on the latter and put it on the book's stylesheet. In the rare instance when there is no reference in the stylebooks or dictionary that seems appropriate, you and your editors may create your own style. But, remember, be consistent throughout your book.

## Checking facts

Careful editors will sometimes challenge statements that are presented as facts or assumptions. They will ask you to verify the spelling of names (never guess at names). Sometimes, it could be a date that needs checking (such as when an actual event happened), or how something is done.

It doesn't matter if you are writing nonfiction, science fiction, short stories, or a novel. Your details and facts must be accurate or you will lose credibility. If you are writing about a religious group, don't have them eating meat if they are practicing vegetarians. And don't send your characters in a story to DisneyLand before it was built. In short, don't make things up thinking no one will know—somebody will, and your credibility will suffer.

## Getting permissions and giving credit

If your book draws on the writing of other people, or uses artwork or photographs produced by someone else, *you need their permission*—in

A New England publisher commissioned a free-lance writer to write a travel guide about our part of Florida. After the book's publication, the review we read indicated that the writer had either not done enough homework, or perhaps thought nobody would know that some of the restaurants and stores selected for inclusion in the guide had been out of business for more than two years. While it is often said that a bad review is better than no review, we doubt that people will want to purchase a *new* travel guide that has outdated and inaccurate information. The easy way to solve that problem is to double-check facts, including appendix information, before going to press.

One novelist we know featured a professional assassin as his main character. The assassin's weapons of choice were poison darts and lethal wrestling holds. Editor Chester Baum asked for proof that the type of poison described in the book would function as the author had indicated. Once he and the author had resolved that detail (the author *did* know his poisons), the editor questioned how a particular wrestling hold had proved fatal. As it turned out, Baum had wrestled during his school years. So the author, also a wrestler, and the editor walked together through the book's scene and ended up in the described lock.

"Aha," said the delighted Baum. He then understood exactly what the author was attempting to describe and was able to recast the sentences so the action was clear.

Not all editorial sessions are that dramatic. But good editing should question, suggest, and improve.

Get permissions in writing. Pay the necessary fees, if any. Err on the side of caution and respect the work of others.

 If you are relying heavily on the material of others, you may want to check with a copyright attorney for the best current legal advice.

advance of printing the book. This includes your publishing historic, previously unpublished letters, such as Civil War correspondence.

Sometimes getting those permissions isn't easy, but as a courtesy, for professional integrity, and to protect yourself from a possible lawsuit, it is a must. You will want to have the permissions in hand before you get too far along in the publishing process because if someone denies you the use of a photograph, or does not want material quoted, you will have to make changes in your book.

A good packager will insist that you give appropriate credit within the text, or on your copyright page, and next to photographs. We have heard many horror stories from the Big Guys and even from small presses about copyright violations and ensuing problems involving both printed material and artwork. Most photography stores and book manufacturers will not make negatives of any previously printed photographs without having written permission from the original studio or photographer in their files.

Remember, *giving credit* is not the same as *asking permission*. If you are using someone else's work, ask for their permission in writing.

You may want to send your request for permission by certified mail, return receipt requested. That way if your efforts to reach the originator of the work are unsuccessful, your attempts are documented.

If you are commissioning someone to do artwork or your cover design, make sure the artist agrees in writing, *before the job is started*, to do it "for hire." That's to protect you later on from having the artist claim a share of the profits of your book even though you have paid up front for the art. Sometimes the artist will insist on a limited agreement which needs to be renegotiated if you plan to use the design on T-shirts or posters for sale rather than for promotional material for the book.

*The Chicago Manual of Style* includes a valuable section on copyrights and permissions. You should review it and, if you still are not sure, contact an attorney who specializes in intellectual properties law.

## "The blues"

Do all your proofreading and editing *before* you generate your camera-ready copy. Do not plan on doing further proofing from the galley proofs or "bluelines."

The bluelines are a mock-up of your book. They are composed of blueprints of the pages and cover, and are made by placing the negatives from which the printing plates will be made over sheets of blueprint paper, exposing them to light, and developing the prints. The sheets of paper are then folded into signatures, trimmed, stapled and arranged as your book will appear.

The inspection of the blues is your last chance to make sure that everything is placed properly, that the pages are in order, and that the photographs or illustrations are not upside down, flipped or placed over the wrong caption. If you spot a serious typographic error you can correct it, but remember, changes can be very costly at this stage. If the changes are because of errors you have made, such as typos, you will be charged for the corrections.

Usually the blues come in by overnight delivery and often must be returned the same day, also by overnight delivery. If you do not process them in a timely fashion you may cause a delay in the printing schedule. Also, if you make major changes at blueline stage, you probably will delay the delivery of your book because it

will lose its place on the production line and will have to be rescheduled for printing and binding.

A book manufacturer's customer service representative we know gave this explanation of how the charges are determined for author alterations at the blueline stage: If just one word in the blueline is changed, the line of type has to be reset ($1.50); then the new line of type has to be pasted on the page ($1.80); finally the page needs to be reshot, making a new negative ($8.70). The total is $12. Three departments are involved—typesetting, paste-up and camera. That's just for one word on one line of one page! You can see how the cost of your changes at this stage of the printing process can truly give you "the blues."

## Scheduling

Although the issue of schedule is discussed in chapter seven, it is germane to your initial conversations with your book packager. If you are planning to sell through wholesale outlets, such as distributors, you and your packager must know and work with their schedules.

Distributors' catalogs usually come out in January and July for the spring and winter seasons. Know deadlines for getting your ad copy submitted.

Because the cover is usually featured in the ad for your book, you may need to provide a copy of the cover several months ahead of the book's actual production. Therefore, cover decisions may be the first ones you need to make with your packager.

# 3 Do your marketing homework

*Begin with the end—sales—in mind. The day you begin planning your book, you must also begin planning your marketing.*—Helen Hays, director of marketing, Favorite Recipes Press.

SURPRISED THAT THE CHAPTER on marketing comes near the beginning of this book? Authors, especially those who hope for sales through traditional outlets such as bookstores and distributors, should let their marketing plans guide their entire project from inception to publication. While we will discuss some of the topics, such as covers, in other sections of the book, we believe that understanding your customer and your market should guide many of your decisions about the book, from its title to its inside and exterior design. Marketing—reaching the consumer—should be the engine driving many of your decisions.

A simple definition of marketing is: Find out what the public wants, then meet that need with your product. To know what the public wants, you also need to know who will buy or read your book. There are some easy ways to find out.

We believe that your marketing really should begin before the first word is typed. It is much harder to

 Do some basic research by talking to bookstore managers and librarians about your topic ideas. They know the market. Then, write a profile of your expected buyer. Include age, education level, and other relevant details. Is your customer a tourist, or perhaps a grandmother looking for a birthday present? Will price be an important factor? Will your book be an impulse buy, or something a purchaser will seek out because of its topic? The profile will help you and your packager design a book product to fit your market.

find a market for your already written book than it is to research, write and design a book for a specific market that you have targeted in advance.

In our initial conferences with authors and self-publishers, we ask them to describe who they expect to be the buyer and who they expect to be the reader. This information will help determine the cover concept, the title, and the material to be included or deleted during the editing process. The buyer is often the reader, but not always. For example, the book may be written for preschoolers, but its cover and subject matter must appeal to the grandparent or parent who will purchase it. What can you put on the book's cover that will appeal to the projected buyer? How about an endorsement

Nancy Jane Tetzlaff-Berens, owner of Jungle Larry's Caribbean Gardens and Zoological Park, commissioned free-lance writer Sharon Rendell to write about the famous Tetzlaff family and the history of the parks in Naples, Florida and Cedar Point, Ohio. After more than three decades in the business, Nancy Jane ("Safari Jane") knew exactly who the primary buyers of the book would be, how much they would be willing to pay, and what information and pictures would interest the buyer and reader. That keen marketing knowledge, drawn from extensive knowledge of her customers, prompted the addition of twice as many photographs as originally planned for the book. The photograph that was selected for the cover and the book's retail price were also based on her detailed buyer profile. The book has national appeal because of the number of visitors to the park's two locations for the past thirty years and the family's high profile. In addition, the book, *Living With Big Cats: The Story of Jungle Larry, Safari Jane, and David Tetzlaff,* has an ideal, steady market through the park's gift shop when the book is promoted by announcers at the animal shows or by park staff.

Free-lance writer and author Carol Perry tells writers groups that once she has an idea for a magazine article, such as a fascinating but unpromoted travel spot, she will rewrite her story several times, fitting the needs of a health magazine, an airline magazine, and a travel magazine. She knows what the editors of each magazine want and she develops her story accordingly. It's a good strategy. In ten years Carol has written and sold seven books, a stage play, and hundreds of nonfiction articles.

by a well-known educator or child psychologist?

Knowing your buyer is as important as knowing who will read your book. Will a woman select it for a female friend? A son for his father? Will someone choose it because it tells how to successfully change careers? Or is it for the middle-aged klutz who wants a simple guide to home repairs? Identifying your reader will help you make decisions about format and content. If your expected reader is a busy parent or time-challenged executive, your material must be easily digestible, not an academic tome.

Professional free-lance writers understand marketing. They research topics that are current then write about them, often tailoring the basic information to several sources or buyers. For example, Sharon Rendell, author of *Living with Big Cats* may well be able to use her interviews and research for use in magazine articles. One might focus on Southwest Florida, where Caribbean Gardens is located; another article might be sold to a magazine for domestic cat owners; another to a travel magazine and another to a trade magazine for animal trainers. Or she may be able to write a second book using material she could not accommodate in the first book. Developing a reader profile will help appropriately focus her material to each situation.

Other authors may write a series of shorter books based on what would be chapters in a larger book, for a specific market, such as for computer buffs or gardeners.

These writers know their audience and may even have a contract with a publisher to do the series.

## Filling a demand

How do you find out what the public wants? Easy—you ask! Start with your library or local booksellers. Ask all of them what types of books they purchase. You will probably find out that at this point they are not investing much in fiction or poetry, especially if it is produced by unknown writers. But, for several years they have been telling us that they *are* looking for how-to-do-it books, self-help books that are constructive (not whiny or vindictive), unusual travel ideas, ethnic books, including biographies and histories, and children's literature that represents diversity or multicultural themes. Regional and local topics are popular with booksellers and regional distributors, such as the news services that stock racks at airports or newsstands, even though distributors can be difficult to deal with.

Our home is in Florida and we have been told repeatedly by bookstore owners that they can't find enough well-produced books about Florida for the state or regional sections of their stores. Why do they want them? Tourists and new residents want to read all they can about our area, either while they are sunbathing or to take home as a souvenir. We do the same thing when we travel—we are always looking for informative books about the places we visit.

Regional topics may include fiction, poetry, history, humor, cookbooks, or guidebooks. They may be about fishing, recreation, or the flora and fauna of a particular area. Or they might focus on a famous resident or even a popular tourist spot. "Local" can mean that the author is local or that the subject matter is of local or regional interest, such as a seafood cookbook, a guide to shells or shorebirds, a town history.

Joan Roethler, owner of the Upstart Crow in Key West looks for new books that fit into the theme of her store—either Key West, or Caribbean themes (such as how to sail to the Bahamas). The book's appearance is important and it must be professional. "Some self-publishers seem to think that the only thing that matters is the content of the book, not its look. But that's not true," she says. She also wants to see how a book and its author can be tied into promotional events in the store.

Kate and Philip Armitage, managers of the popular MacIntosh Books and Music Shop in Sanibel, Florida, will tell you that they have three main criteria for selecting titles by new authors: Is it local? Is the price right? Is the cover eye-catching?

"If we don't buy a new book outright, we might take a few copies on consignment, to see if there is a market for the book," says Philip.

"It's good for authors to pop in once in awhile," Kate told us, "to remind us about their books and to see if we should reorder."

This is good advice because independent stores are often not set up for automatic reorder as your book sells.

To put it bluntly, the public creates the demand for books.

Writers who fill that demand with a professional product, and aggressively market their book, will find outlets in the marketplace.

## Titles must be right

Your title is an important part of your marketing strategy. Make it work for you. Get feedback on it from your friends and from professionals. Be open to change based on their suggestions.

Titles can sell the book, or they can be misleading or even offensive. If you are writing a self-help book about divorce, don't call it *My Life with the Spouse from Hell.* Turn the title into something more positive, something that other people can relate to and won't feel embarrassed to have on their coffee table. You may end up with much of the same content, but you

 Keep your title short or put the key elements first if you want it to fit into the microfiche entry and computer systems used by distributors and libraries. These systems typically contain room for only thirty characters. An abbreviated version of the title won't make sense to someone perusing the list for titles about a specific topic.

might find better sales results calling your book *Six Tips for Coping with an Abusive Partner,* or *How to Divorce Without Upsetting the Children.*

Next to the design of your cover, your title must deliver the punch that says, "Buy me!"

During a segment of "All Things Considered" on National Public Radio[7], host Robert Siegel interviewed author André Bernard who had just published a book about titles. The book, aptly titled, *Now, All We Need is a Title,* tells what some of the great books were originally called. For example, *Gone with the Wind* was first titled *Tote the Weary Load,* and Alex Haley's *Roots* was first termed *Before This Anger. Valley of the Dolls* was titled as *They Don't Build Statues to Businessmen.* Bernard noted that, fortunately for several authors, including Margaret Mitchell, the publisher, or maybe a friend, intervened for the better before press time.

You will miss sales opportunities if your title is too cute or too vague. Your book may be overlooked by a regional buyer because you have not mentioned the region the book is about in your title or subtitle. Or your title may have meaning to you, but fails completely to tell a buyer what the book is about. Don't title your nonfiction book *Booze City,* if it has nothing to do with alcohol. Don't call your book *Tiptoeing Through the Woodlands* if you are retelling the story of Daniel Boone. At least mention his name—*with Daniel Boone.*

Consider the impact of each word in your title. Certain words appeal to specific markets; others may turn them off. For example, *My Life with the Spouse from Hell* could be written by a very sincere and religious person, but the word "hell," while perhaps aptly describing the marital situation, could turn off other folks who would not use the "H" word, or might be uncomfortable with the intensity of the implied emotion. If your book is of a very personal nature, you will have to decide if you are writing simply to ventilate and vindicate, or if you really have a message beyond your own situation. When you have decided, title it accordingly.

Bookstores and distributors carry many more types of books than have been described above. You will improve your chances of success in the traditional market if you find out *before* you write your book what subjects will sell.

Unfortunately, most writers do not ask, much less answer, the marketing questions before sitting down at the typewriter or computer. Most have begun with an idea for a poem or story. They write it. They may even illustrate it before they seek an outlet for the results of their creativity. Often they are disappointed that nobody is buying what they have labored so long to produce.

### Dealing with the "obvious"

Occasionally the answers to the basic marketing questions seem obvious, other times not. For example, the one of the first questions we ask people who have written a children's story or picture book is: "For what age child have you written your book?" Surprisingly, most writers aren't sure, even though they already have completed the story.

The age of the reader is critical to the presentation of the material. Books for young children use a lot of color inside and out. But the picture-book appearance would not appeal to upper-elementary school students. Volunteers in the Reading is Fundamental Program tell us that upper elementary students like "chapter books"— books divided into chapters. Reading a book with chapters is a milestone showing that these preteens want to identify themselves with the adult rather than with the picture-book market.

Other questions we ask: How difficult is the vocabulary? Are challenging words a plus for parents who may want their children to enrich their language skills? Does the book have a message? Has this book been "done" a million times? If so, yours needs to have a different twist or it won't compete well with the other books in the stores.

### Ask the experts

Beginning, and even professional writers who are serious about publishing books for children can easily get good marketing feedback on the appropriateness of the material to various age groups as well as the book's overall salability, by taking two very simple steps.

First make some copies of your manuscript and give it to families with children to read and critique. Children love to give advice. Take their opinions seriously. Did they think the beginning needs to have more action? Could they tell you what the book was about? Did they like the characters and find them interesting? Ask each child-reader what age group would best like the book. Kids know.

Next, take your materials to a bookstore and to the library. Look at what the competition will be for your book. Talk to the staff and ask them if your idea has possibilities, then listen to what all these experienced resource people tell you. Their answers will be constructive, and will help guide your publishing decisions.

### Other considerations

Traditionally, self-publishers have sold their books through bookstores and to libraries. These outlets are still an important part of today's options but they may be less important than they have been in the past. Most book experts counsel that you should *not* expect your best sales from bookstores. Remember that the Big Guys are sinking huge dollars into national campaigns. There are more than fifty thousand new titles published every year, and that's a lot of books from which to pick, and a lot of competition for your title. When you are making your initial decisions about your market, consider these alternatives:

✓ sales through catalogs
✓ sales through direct mail (mailing lists)
✓ sales through seminars (give a talk and sell your books)
✓ sales through talk shows
✓ sales through the Internet

Will your topic appeal to a specific segment of the population? Do you know if there are clubs or organizations with a particular interest in your subject? For example, self-publisher Donald Moyer Wilson knew that books about Amelia Earhart have a ready audience. His marketing for *Amelia Earhart: Lost Legend* (Enigma

Self-published author Joe Sabah of Denver, Colorado, is making money twice from his "how to" book. Sabah came up with a unique idea to help his just-out-of-high-school son land his first job in a tight job market. He wrote a "sales letter" talking about what his son *could do*, instead of what he *had done*. It worked! Sabah developed his idea called the "Gold Form" (after the goldenrod paper on which it was printed) into a book, *How to Get the Job You Really Want and Get Employers to Call You*. Except for a few copies at a local bookstore, Sabah has sold his book exclusively on radio talk shows. Speaking from his home, he talks to audiences all over the country, offering a money-back guarantee on the book. Orders have poured in through his 800 number. After five years, and more than 582 talk shows, Sabah says he has sold almost 23,000 copies at full price. That's $330,000 worth of books!

The second way he has made money from his book is by developing a system written about in his second book called *How to Get on Radio Talk Shows All Across America Without Leaving Your Home or Office*. He markets the idea along with a list of shows and the names of the persons to contact. And of course, he sells both his book and his list when he is *paid* to speak at seminars. (See Appendix B.)

Press) is appropriately targeted at Earhart researchers, Earhart society members, the media, aviation buffs, and even members of Zonta International, of which Earhart was a member. In addition to other media, Don Wilson's book has been reviewed in the Earhart Society newsletter, and he sells his book during talks he gives around

Florida real estate broker Phil Wilson self-published a book titled, *How to Appraise, Buy and Sell a Business.* He sells the book exclusively through seminars he conducts and by word of mouth. The book is set up with occasional workbook-style pages, making its use very personal and therefore not likely to be shared. Phil is successful in his sales and continues to reprint and update his material regularly. He's found a niche and tied his product in with a guaranteed market, namely his own seminar.

Rose Sims, a Methodist minister, once was assigned to a small church threatened with closing. However, she turned the church into a thriving, dynamic congregation. She has put her crusade to reopen American's small rural churches into a successful self-published book, *The Dream Lives On.* She conducts church-growth seminars and sells her book at these forums. She has a dramatic story to tell, a good product and a ready market.

Take a look at your material. Can you create a package with your book, yourself, and tapes or videos? Does your topic lend itself to promotion on radio talk shows or to direct mail sales? Identify potential audiences to target, and go after them.

the country. Because it was packaged properly, it was available for distribution nationwide, and was in its second printing within six months. To stimulate sales, Wilson also sends out direct-mail fliers and teaches a class about Earhart.

In planning your book, consider how you will let the potential buyers know about it through mail, talk shows, or seminars.

Ann Rust, Joe Sabah, Phil Wilson, Donald Moyer Wilson, and Rose Sims are only five of many examples of writers who have found a market niche and filled it. Some use seminars and talk shows to sell their books, often including the price of their book in the seminar fee. This technique guarantees sales.

## You can market a book by its cover

You many not be able to judge a book by its cover, but you sure can use the cover to sell the book! Part of your preliminary marketing planning will include determining the elements you will use in the design of your cover. While we will be discussing cover design later, consider this: Your cover is an advertisement for your book. In fact, for those who are not specifically seeking your book, the cover is the single most effective advertisement you have.

Richard Capps, director of product development for Unique Books, Inc., a library distributor that distributes for many small and independent publishers, says that new nonfiction books are not necessarily selected for their content (no buyer has time to read them all), but for their cover and title. Their salespeople, like those of other distributors, do not carry thousands of books with them when they call on libraries—they carry book covers. Ron Watson, book buyer at Ingram Books, says the cover must be able to sell the book within seven seconds.

Librarians and buyers for bookstores will also judge your

 Always order an overprint of your cover so you have enough to give each salesperson at each distributor. Several hundred extra covers is a good number. If you don't you may be asked to submit twenty books to the distributor. The covers will then be removed from them for the salespeople to carry with them on the road. There is no point in wasting good copies of your books.

 To save money on your second printing, if you anticipate one, have enough covers and jackets printed as an overrun of the first printing to use on the second. Store them flat and do not have them trimmed. Remember, it is less expensive to keep the press running than to set it up a second time, especially if you have a four-color cover.

 Cover! Cover! Cover! You *must* have a professional cover! This sermon is preached by every distributor and book buyer. According to Chris Pearl, of Pearl and Associates, look for these credentials: A graphic artist who has a well-rounded background, such as a classical fine arts degree, and at least a decade of successful experience in book cover design.

book by the cover and your title.

The colors, choice of typeface, the design elements and layout can be critical to a sale. Professional cover designers know what makes a dynamic cover, and they know how the combined elements convey a

message to make your book look like other books in its category, or like no other book in its genre.

If you consider the cover as a billboard or advertisement for the book, then use it to sell the book. In addition to the artistic elements incorporated in the cover, and the title itself, you may need to include a subtitle to give the reader some additional information about the book's content.

### Endorsements as advertising

Getting experts, influential people, or people with important (and relevant) careers to comment on your book can be a powerful selling point. Their "blurbs"— placed prominently on the front or back cover—will lend credibility to your book and may help talk a potential buyer into making the purchase.

Endorsements can be important no matter what the subject of your book is. Suppose you have written a nonfiction book about divorce, or child abuse or gardening. If you are not recognized as an authority

 Don't be afraid to write blurbs and send them off to the persons you want to sign them. If they are willing to endorse your book, they will write their own sentences, possibly based on your suggestions, or approve what you have provided.

in your subject matter, but know your material is accurate and comprehensive, get people with credentials or name recognition to read it and lend their support through an endorsement. To meet your deadlines, start gathering endorsements before the book is completed by letting potential endorsers read an early draft or chapter outline.

Even if you, the author, are well known, endorsements will help make sales. If you are an entertainer who has written an autobiog-

raphy, don't hesitate to call on fellow show-biz colleagues to be quoted as saying something like, "Great backstage stories," or, "A page-turner. I couldn't put it down." Or, "Authoritative in the field." Their names will help sell.

If your previous material has been favorably reviewed, work that into your back cover, jacket flaps, or front matter. If your book wins a prize, have foil stickers printed stating the award information and affix them to the cover of each copy you send out. Don't be shy about promoting yourself!

### The price must be right

The retail price of your book is a very important part of your marketing considerations. Compare the prices of books like yours at the bookstore. If they are selling for $12.95, certainly you would not want to price your book at $25.95. Consumers probably wouldn't buy it at that price unless you have produced something really special.

Big Guys usually price their products at seven- to-nine times the unit production cost, but because they are printing in such large quantities, the unit production cost is quite low. It is very difficult for the small publisher or self-publisher to afford to do a large enough press run to put a reasonable, competitive price on the product, and still be able to make a profit when the books are discounted to distributors, wholesalers or to bookstores (See Chapter 7 for an in-depth discussion of discount schedules.)

We recommend that you try to balance the size of your press run, the size of your wallet, and the "sticker" price of your book— taking into consideration the way you expect to sell it, through wholsalers or at retail. If you do this carefully you should be able to at least break even on your production costs when you have sold about half of the first printing. Many authors choose to only do a short first run and deliberately price their books at very close to cost in the hope that with good sales, they will be able attract a major publisher or perhaps an agent. If they don't, when they sell out they will have just about broken even anyway.

Your marketing costs will also cut into your profit, but in the long run, if you plan carefully, you should be able to recoup your investment or even make a profit.

Your packager can give you assistance in pricing your book.

## Small markets

Perhaps your material is of more limited interest, such as a book of poetry, personal philosophy, or maybe even a family history. How you package your book will depend on your pocketbook and your potential audience. If you anticipate selling one hundred copies of a clan history to family members at a reunion, and perhaps a few more to friends or to the local bookstore, you will want to make your packaging or printing decisions on that basis. Many poets test the market for their work by having a chapbook printed. They are typically low-budget productions with one-color covers, but need not look that way if time is taken to have the book set up properly and proof read carefully. They are not likely to reach a wide commercial market, but satisfy the author's need to have poems in bound form.

If you aren't sure about how extensive the market is for your material, take samples of it to a bookstore or library. Then listen carefully to what is being said about the market. A small press run will get you into print, with the satisfaction of having a book. If you are realistic about the demand for your product, you won't have 10,000 copies produced and then find out too late that nobody is buying that type of book or that you do not have the marketing resources or stamina to sell it.

You might also consider testing the market by having your work published in a cooperative poetry or literature anthology. In a cooperative anthology, each contributor shares in the cost of the produc-

 Massachusetts poet, Nancy Miller, has seen how self-publishing can bring success. She began by publishing selected poems in two cooperative anthologies.[8] "First, there was a flurry of press about the anthology, and people beyond my friends and family began to see me as as a poet. I was invited to judge a poetry contest for the *Lawrence Eagle-Tribune* and subsequently was asked to be a part of some poetry readings. As a result, a local free-lance writer interviewed me for an article in an insert to our weekly regional newspaper. My circle of author acquaintances and friends widened, leading to new knowledge of writing workshops which I was able to attend.

"As my visibility increased, I began to take myself as a poet more seriously. I felt the confidence to submit my work to various publications and contests. After the national magazine, *Mediphors,* accepted one of my poems in 1994, I submitted to other journals and anthologies. Although there were maybe forty rejection slips for each success, I was committed to sharing my work. In April 1996, the anthology, *Our Mothers, Our Selves,* published by Bergin & Garvey, printed one of my poems alongside works by Robert Bly, Maya Angelou, Maxine Kumin and Sharon Olds. Elated and validated, I am even more committed to sharing my voice."

Miller has now decided to self-publish *Dance Me Along the Path,*[9] an entire volume of her own work. "I prefer to self-publish so that I can retain the control (on one occasion one of my poems appeared in a newsletter with the critical last line missing), both artistically and financially. I have seen chapbooks of disappointing quality and I know fine poets who suffer commercial rejection again and again. Walt Whitman's first printing of *Leaves of Grass,* was self-published; sometimes editors misjudge good material."

tion of the book. When the book is published, each participant receives a share of the press run in proportion to the share of the costs they underwrote.

Cooperative anthologies should be fully credentialed for retail sales. These anthologies are a relatively inexpensive method of having your work published. Not only are these anthologies a good means of getting your work in print, they are an invaluable opportunity for you to develop your marketing abilities and salesmanship.

## Marketing checklist

Professional book publicists and agents know that marketing must begin *before* the book is published. Among the elements for you to consider while developing a marketing plan[10]:

✓ Look: Title, pricing, jacket or cover concept, overall format and page design.

✓ Positioning: Who is the buyer? The reader? The distributor? The bookseller? The reviewer?

✓ Publicity: The "must" review; media; targeted media, press release as book review, local area publicity opportunities, and never forget word-of-mouth, the best publicity of all.

✓ Sales: Specialty retailers or wholesalers not covered by your distributor, order forms, representation at national and regional trade shows and other conventions.

✓ Subsidiary rights: Serial, syndication, book clubs, foreign rights, paperback, electronic.

Early on, before your book is released, a consultation with an experienced book-marketing firm could be a tremendous benefit for exposure and sales.

# 4 Creating a professional product

*If we want the same treatment that the big publishers get, we need to act like professional publishers. Instead of bucking the system, we must learn to fit into the professional publishing community.* —Christopher Carroll, sales manager, McGuinn & McGuire, and vice-president of the Florida Publishers Association[11]

YOU'VE PROBABLY HEARD the old expression "penny-wise and pound-foolish." We want you to know that applied to book packaging, the value of this age-old caution is more than sound. You can have a brilliant idea and a terrific story, but if you skimp on the costs of book production, or ignore the traditional setup of a book, you may well doom your entire product to failure.

Producing a book is similar to selling a house. The house may be structurally sound, but if it lacks "curb appeal" because the outside is a mess and the inside is weird, it won't fare well against the competition.

Books, like all products, must meet certain standards to compete in the marketplace. There are, unfortunately, many self-published books that by their very look proclaim that they are "homemade."

Don't get us wrong. There are times that the homemade look may not matter very much—for instance, when a self-publishing author on a very limited budget anticipates a very limited readership. People will purchase the book because they know the author, or perhaps because there is a local angle, such as a town history, or because the book is produced by a local writers club for its members. Or, the book may be simply a family history.

A construction-paper or cardstock cover, printed in one color and handbound over a book that has been photocopied from typewritten copy, might be all right for some book projects, but remember, aside from a possible "courtesy" placement by a local independent bookstore, it won't be widely salable.

Some authors think they can be successful by simply taking copy they have generated on their computer or typewriter directly to the printer instead of having their work professionally prepared. They may have done the cover design themselves or perhaps have had a friend draw something. In the end, they have a book in hand, but because they have taken the least expensive route and have declined professional guidance, their book looks amateurish inside and out.

Lack of salability should not come as a surprise to them.

We believe it is just as easy, and not much more expensive, to make a book look good as it is to allow it to be done with an unprofessional appearance. Working with a book packaging service will ensure that you will deal with all the significant components necessary to produce a quality book.

Gene Starner, a regional buyer for Barnes & Noble, underscores the need for books to be professionally produced, fully credentialed, properly priced, and available through a wholesaler in order to be carried by any of the one thousand mall locations of B. Dalton Booksellers, and superstores such as Barnes & Noble, Borders/Walden or Books-A-Million. Only if a book meets the basic standards, both inside and out, can it be considered for its subject matter.

**What are credentials?**

The first things your book needs are the proper credentials. Credentials are the "fingerprints" of your book, making it identifiable and salable. If you have any plans to market your book to stores, libraries, catalogs, or distributors, you must have it credentialed. Without credentials, you will have as much luck as if you are trying to show a mutt at the Westminster Kennel Club. The most important credential is your International Standard Book Number or ISBN. The ISBN system is voluntary, but has been adopted internationally by virtually all publishers, distributors and bookstores.

Your ISBN is a unique number consisting of ten digits, that identifies your book. An ISBN is never recycled; it is permanently assigned to a specific version of a book. Each version of your book (hardcover, softcover, disk, or tape) will have its own ISBN.

ISBNs are issued to publishers by the R. R. Bowker Company in groups of ten or one hundred or more, depending on the expected number of publications per year. The ISBNs are then assigned in ascending numerical order by the publisher from the list to their books.

By agreement between Bowker and publishers, the ISBN must be printed on the verso, or copyright page, and on the lower right-hand corner of the outside back cover. Bowker now suggests that the ISBN also be printed on the spine.

This book's ISBN is 1-881539-14-8. The first digit represents the country of origin, the United States. The second group of six digits is the publisher's prefix, identifying Tabby House as the publisher. The third pair, 14, tells which book this is in the sequence of books Tabby House has published using this particular "bank" or group of ISBNs. The final number is a "check" number which mathematically proves that the rest of the number is valid.

Bowker also publishes *Forthcoming Books in Print*, and *Books in Print*—comprehensive listings that provide pertinent information about books to book buyers.

Books-A-Million store manager Bobbi Larson tells us that the credentials are very important if customers want to order a book. The ISBN will let the store track a book back to a publisher. Without the ISBN, sales are easily lost.

**Bar code**

Like the ISBN, the EAN Bookland bar code contains important information which is particularly useful to stores for point of sale information. When the bar code is scanned or entered into the computerized cash register, in addition to the price and tax coming up on the register, the appropriate inventory control information is entered into the system. In some cases the systems are part of the store's distribution inventory system, and will even automatically reorder from the distributor.

The bar code is a series of vertical bars encoded with the title, ISBN, and sometimes the price of your book. Bar codes are usually produced as a negative and are provided to the cover designer on film or disk to be incorporated directly into the composite film for the convenience of the printer. The bar code typically is printed on the back cover of a softcover book and on the jacket of a hardcover edition.

It's easy to get a bar code produced. There are many bar code services (See Appendix B.) which make them up for about twenty-five dollars, and can get them to you very quickly. Some book manufacturers and cover designers also have the equipment to produce them for you at low cost. The bar code is an essential part of the credentials package. Some distributors and bookstores now refuse books that do not have a bar code. Use it to look professional and, more importantly, to enhance the book's salability in retail outlets.

## Copyright, Library of Congress Catalog Card Number and CIP

The rest of your credentials are located on the copyright or the verso page. All left-hand pages are verso pages, but *the* verso page is the one on the back of the title page. You should also put the book's credentials on the back cover. Right-hand pages are called "recto" pages.

Under 1984 copyright laws, your work is copyrighted to you as soon as you put the words on paper. You don't need to have your book officially registered with the copyright office prior to publication. In fact, if you do, it will make things a bit more complicated, as

 We have seen self-published books in which authors actually print on the verso page, "Library of Congress Number pending" or some such silly thing. Perhaps the authors didn't understand how to get the credentials they need, or why they are important.

you will have to explain why you are trying to copyright the same material twice. If you are concerned about your copyright, put the copyright symbol, ©, the year, and your name on the bottom of each manuscript page.

Your packager will see to it that your copyright notice is printed on the verso page. Once the book is off the press, you or your packager should fill out the copyright application (Form TX) and send it, along with the twenty-dollar fee and two copies of the book to the Register of Copyrights at the Library of Congress.

If you are selling the rights to your book or working with a subsidy publisher or vanity press, be sure to resolve the issue of who will hold the copyright *before* you sign the contract. Once your book is published it is too late and you may find that, after you have paid for the entire production of your book, you no longer own the copyright.

The year of publication must coincide with the year of copyright. Distributors and buyers unfortunately make the assumption that if the copyright year is not the current year, that the material is old and should be on the "backlist." The backlist refers to releases from

Manufactured in the United States of America
Library of Congress Catalog Card Number: 95–35376
ISBN: 1–881539–03–2
Illustrations: Christopher Grotke
Page design: Abigail Grotke
Cover design: Pearl and Associates
Setup and typography: Bob Lefebvre

**Library of Congress Cataloging-in-Publication Data**
Salisbury, Linda G. (Linda Grotke)
    Smart self-publishing : an author's guide to producing a
marketable book / Linda and Jim Salisbury : with foreword by Joe Sabah.
            p.   cm.
    "Hot tips, sound advice, and publishing adventures from authors,
distributors, librarians, and book buyers."
    Includes index.
    ISBN 1–881539–03–2
    1. Self-publishing --United States.   I. Salisbury, Jim, 1936–
II. Title.
Z289.5.S25   1995
070.5'93--dc20                                        95–35376

 Tabby House
4429 Shady Lane
Charlotte Harbor, Florida, 33980
(941) 629-7646

*The verso page of our first edition shows the information that must be included.*

If your book is going to be delivered in December, you might think about delaying its release by a few weeks or a month in order to use the new year's copyright rather than the old, thus extending the life of your book as a "new" publication. Remember, printing is not the same as publication. Your book is *published* when it is made available to the public and that date is the date used for copyright.

previous years that are still available from a distributor, but are not actively promoted or displayed. You can update the copyright if you make significant changes in your book for a second edition.

The Library of Congress offers two services to authors. Both must be initiated *before* your book is published. The one used by most self-publishing authors and many small presses is called the Preassigned Number Program. Authors and publishers fill out an application that describes the upcoming book. The application is reviewed by the Library of Congress office and, if all is in order, a Library of Congress Catalog Card Number is issued to the publisher.

It usually takes between two and three weeks to get your Library of Congress Catalog Card Number, so don't wait until the last minute. You will need to have this number printed in your book on the verso page for catalog cards in libraries. Obviously, you cannot get a *pre*assigned number *after* the book is printed.

The second, called the Cataloging in Publication (CIP) Program, is used for books that are expected to be widely used in libraries.

There is a lengthy application to be filled out, and either all or a significant portion of the book must be submitted for review.

If you, as a publisher, are registered with the CIP program and the book fits the criteria, you will receive CIP data to print on the verso page, *exactly as provided.* CIP data is sent to libraries on microfiche and is duplicated on library cards for catalogs, making the librarian's job easier.

Self-publishers and one-book publishers are not accepted for the CIP program, but some book manufacturers and some library distributors will do CIP for you for a small fee. This is a big help if you do not qualify for the governmental program. Use their services if you want to have the CIP cataloging information to print on your book's verso page. Obviously, CIP can help you make your book more attractive to the library market.

Remember, after your book is finished and you have copies in hand, you or your packager will need to send one copy to the Library of Congress and two copies, with the appropriate fee and completed application, to the copyright office.

## About your book's cover

What is the first thing you notice about a book? For most people it is the cover, front, back, and spine. It's surprising, though, how many do-it-yourself self-publishers have only the front cover printed. The spine and back are blank.

Richard Capps, of Unique Books, a library distribution service, tells us what goes into his selection of new titles to present to librarians across the country: "I look at the cover, the quality of the binding and to see if the book has a table of contents, index, and cataloging in publication. I'll open it up and pull on the book rather aggressively to determine if its binding will withstand the library circulation."

Capps notes that librarians, faced with making selections from as many as 2,300 titles in the salesperson's catalog, and looking at many covers, in only two- to-three hours may not have time even to read the data slip accompanying the book's cover.

What does sell the book? "Covers, covers, covers and titles. Does the book look professionally done? The cover is what catches your eye, and it is what catches the librarian's eye," says Capps.

## Cover design

Book cover design is itself a specialty field, and within it cover designers are often known for individual specialties. Some may be very good at science fiction covers, or medical/textbook covers, children's books, or romance novels, for example.

You will need to have an eye-catching cover that is mainstream for your type of book, and that usually means giving up your own design ideas and Cousin Ella's art.

Your book packager should have a number of professional designers either on staff or available as freelancers. Or you can get names of professional designers from publishers' associations. Professional cover artists will be able to create a well-designed cover to fit every budget and every book.

After consulting with you, your book packager will also give direction to the artist by discussing the overall concept of the book and its title, and perhaps suggest some elements to be used, such as photographs. You or your packager should give the designer several chapters to read to help stimulate subject-oriented ideas. The cover designer should submit two or three sketches or concepts for your consideration. You should have an opportunity to see these and choose between, or combine elements from the options. Don't make your packager and artist try to read your mind. If you have a vision of what your cover should look like, share it.

We suggest that you first go to a bookstore and look to see what type of covers new books in your genre (with the current year's copyright) are featuring. You want your book to be striking, but also to fit in with the other books on the shelf. Then listen to the professionals you have hired. Had we dictated what we thought this book's cover should be like, we never would have ended up with our designer's brilliant concept. We gave him an idea of what we wanted the book to do for us, and turned him loose. The result has been a winner, catching the eyes of reviewers, experts in the field of publishing, and book buyers.

Authors can run up production costs and lose time if they fail to communicate their ideas until after preliminary designs are completed, then trying to micromanage the project. If you have hired professionals, let them do their job.

Since you are paying for expertise, listen to the experts. But, if you absolutely hate a particular color, let your packager know so the artist does not inadvertently come up with a color scheme that will make you say, "Yeech!" Keep in mind, though, "Yeech!" may be the best color to sell the book.

Unless you are a professional cover designer, chances are that you should trust the professional's layout, colors and design. Book-cover designers know what works in the marketplace and what composes a good cover for your book.

Your book's back cover is a full-page advertisement, and it is really important that you make full use of it. There are certain elements you need to include: the retail price, the bar code, the ISBN, and the imprint of the publisher (name and/or logo). In addition, you should supply your packager with endorsements, a concise and compelling description of the content, and, if you think it will help sales, a photo of yourself and your biographical information.

And don't laugh at this reminder: Don't forget to have your name put on the cover. We have actually seen some books printed without the author's name! But unless you are very well-known, don't make your name the focal point—a good design will sell the book even if your name won't.

The spine is an important part of any book's professional look and its marketability. It needs to have the book's title and the author's name on it, the publisher's imprint and maybe the ISBN It should

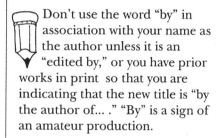

 Librarians recommend that when you design your spine, leave room at the bottom for librarians to stick on cataloging information without covering important information.

Don't use the word "by" in association with your name as the author unless it is an "edited by," or you have prior works in print so that you are indicating that the new title is "by the author of... ." "By" is a sign of an amateur production.

also make a dramatic visual statement, so when the book is shelved spine out, as nine out of ten books are, the color and the title have a better chance to catch the attention of browsers.

To sum up, there are hundreds, if not thousands of books in the typical bookstore, and if your book is to sell, it must be competitive. The average buyer, unless on a specific mission to buy a particular book, must be drawn to your cover. If bookstore browsers pick up your book it is because the front cover, the spine, or the title has caught their eye. After looking at the front cover, they usually flip the book over and look at the back cover and read the blurbs. Your book needs to be screaming, "Read me!" If the title and covers have done their job, potential buyers will probably look at the dust jacket flaps or leaf through the book for additional information. Most impulse decisions are made in just a few seconds. Check out your own book-buying habits. Ask your friends what factors make them decide to buy an "unknown" book.

## Between the covers

If you are like most people, you have been reading books all your life without giving much more than cursory thought to book format. A half-title page? What's that?

For your self-published book to compete in the marketplace of bookstores and libraries, you must include in it all the relevant, traditional elements of books. It is important that you hire experts, either on your own or through your book packager, to do those things that are outside of your expertise, such as formatting, cover and page design, typesetting and indexing.

For a detailed explanation of the anatomy of a book, we recommend reading *The Chicago Manual of Style*. Meanwhile, here are some of the basics which you should know. Between the covers there are three distinct sections: the front matter, the body of the book, and the back matter. Depending on the book's purpose, the content of each of those sections will vary. A novel is not likely to need an index, but may have a lengthy introduction.

The front matter has page numbers printed in italic Roman numerals (except for any blank or "white" pages, which do not have any numbers or headers on them). The front matter usually includes a half-title page, which has only the title (no subtitle or author's name), which is often used for autographs. It is followed by a white page, then the recto title page, which is more comprehensive. The title page includes the title, subtitle, author's and/or editor's name, the name of the person who has written the foreword and the publisher. It is followed by *the* verso page with credential information, including copyright, ISBN, Library of Congress Catalog Card Number, Cataloging in Publication data, printing history and permissions. You also can use the verso page to give credit to the cover designers, illustrators, and others.

The verso page is followed by the dedication, a blank page, contents page(s), list of illustrations or tables if applicable; foreword, preface, acknowledgments, introduction. Try to start each new section on a recto page.

The foreword (not forward) should be written by some knowledgeable person *other than the author*. The author's preface includes reasons why the book was written. The introduction includes information which should be read and understood before delving into the main body of the book.

The body of the book includes the text which usually is divided into chapters and/or sections. Care must be taken to establish adequate margins and white space so that the pages do not look overcrowded. A rule of thumb is to have about 35 percent white space on each page. That would include the margins and the area between lines of type called leading (pronounced "ledding").

You may also want running heads or footers on the pages which will identify the title of the book, chapter, topic covered on the page, or the author, and you will need to decide where you want to place the page numbers. Later in this chapter we will expand on book setup and other considerations such as choice of type styles and sizes.

The back matter is found after the body of the book and usually includes the appendix, endnotes, glossary, bibliography or reference list, index and perhaps a page about the author. Each section has its own specific rules which are defined and described at length in *The Chicago Manual of Style*.

## Index

*All* nonfiction books should be indexed. The fact that the book is indexed is extremely important to librarians and to the Library of Congress Cataloging in Publication division—to say nothing of your readers. A proper index adds credibility to your book.

Creating an index is not as easy as it may seem even though many computer word-processing programs include an indexing func-

tion. A truly comprehensive index may require as much as an hour of work for each five pages of text, *after* the indexer has become familiar with the book. We recommend a thorough reading of the indexing section of *The Chicago Manual of Style*, and perhaps the retention of a professional indexer to do the work.

## Your book's dimensions

In selecting the size of your book, you need to consider the following:

✓ Economy. Use a standard size page so that after the signatures are printed, folded and trimmed you are not wasting vast amounts of paper. Odd-size books or unusual paper stocks add significantly to the cost of producing your book.

✓ The size of other books dealing with the same general subject.

✓ The ultimate weight of your book, or its handling ease.

Mass market paperbacks, such as pulp westerns and mysteries, and even the paperback editions of best-selling novels, can have press runs of hundreds of thousands. They are printed by "web" presses like those that newspapers are printed on. The paper used, a type of newsprint, comes on huge rolls and is not readily available for small print jobs, and the size of those books is not the most economical size for small press runs.

The fiction and nonfiction books sold in bookstores are referred to as "trade" books. Most trade books are printed on "sheet-fed" presses which use stacks of precut sheets of paper much like a copy machine does. These sheets are precut in certain sizes based on the sizes of the pages commonly used in books. Using the standard sizes will save money.

You usually will find that 5½-by-8½, 6-by-9, or 7-by-10 inches, are the most cost-effective page sizes for trade books. These sizes conform to book standards. A coffee-table book, with lots of pictures, will probably be 8½-by-11, or 8-by-10 inches.

If your book is very lengthy, you could consider reducing the thickness by increasing the size of the pages, changing to a lighter-weight paper, or even publishing in two volumes. You can also reduce the number of pages through font selection or leading changes. But don't sacrifice readability in the process.

## Photographs and choice of paper

If you plan to have photographs in your book, try to use professional glossy prints, as they reproduce best. But, if you must use home snapshots, try to pick ones with good contrast and no busy backgrounds. Have your photographs properly cropped, sized and halftoned by a professional. The results are worth the expense.

Coated paper stocks such as enamel are much better for photoreproduction than are the common commodity offset papers that most text-only books are printed on. They are also more expensive. Discuss your photo ideas with your packager or with your printer to determine which kind of paper is best for your job. Indicate in the text or margins approximately where the pictures should be placed. We say approximately because sometimes in the typeset version, the spot you indicate will end up in a page position that just won't fit the picture—like a half inch from the bottom of the page. Give your typesetter some leeway in picture placement.

You will need to write a short cutline for each photograph. A cutline, or caption, should tell the picture's story, and identify the people in the picture from left to right. Don't retell the text in the caption.

## Types of bindings and cover materials

Most books that you see on bookstore shelves are bound with what is known as a "perfect" binding. Perfect binding is accomplished by gathering the signatures, trimming off the spine or gutter area, then gluing a paper cover directly to the body of the book. A signature is a group of pages printed on both sides of one flat sheet that has been folded and trimmed. The number of pages in a signature is commonly a multiple of eight, and will depend on the dimensions of the book and the size of the press. Perfect binding has a squared-off look and is quite economical. This book has a perfect binding.

Perfect-bound books usually are simply glued together, but sometimes are "smyth sewn," a process in which the signatures are stitched together with strong nylon thread for added durability. Casebound, or hardcover books are almost always smyth sewn.

Pamphlets, small guidebooks or other books with fewer than fifty pages or so usually have a "saddlestitch" binding. The cover is folded around the text, then stapled or stitched to the pages. The signatures are trimmed top and bottom and outside but not on the spine.

Gene Starner evaluates a book's binding when he selects regional titles for the Barnes & Nobles' stores:

"Perfect binding is more expensive [than saddlestitching], but perfect-bound books have the potential for a longer shelf life and better sales because the name of the book can be placed on the spine. Since most of our books are placed on the shelves spine out, stapled or saddlestitched books essentially disappear. Also, many of our stores are not carrying stapled books unless they come with a shelf or counter display."

A hardcover or case-binding will add considerably to the cost per copy of your book. If you have a hard cover you will usually need to have a dust jacket made for it. Bookstores like dust jackets because if there is damage, it is more economical to replace a jacket than an entire book, but dust jackets are expensive, especially if they are printed with four colors.

Some casebound books, such as children's books, textbooks, or coffee-table books, may have the cover design printed on the finished case. Others have a foil-stamped cloth or plastic over the binder board.

There are many types of cover materials to select from for either hardbound or softcover books. Check bookstores and libraries to see what material books of your

 If your book will be sold or stored in areas where there is high humidity, you should specify that it be made with a no-curl cover stock.

kind use. Most paperback cover-stock is 9, 10 or 12 point and coated on one or two sides to help prevent curling. After printing, the cover is treated with film, UV laminate, or varnish to make it glossy and to protect it.

Although the type of binding you select may be based on how much you have to invest in your book, you also need to consider how it will be used. Cookbooks, for instance, are handier if they have a washable cover and lie flat. Many are bound with a plastic spiral binding, which is also called a comb or GBC binding, but bookstores find this type of binding

difficult to store and display, and libraries don't like books with spiral bindings.

Otabind® is a type of perfect binding that is designed to open flat on the reading surface. The cover is not glued to the book's spine, allowing the book to lie flat.

Fishing guide books might hold up better if they are waterproof. *A Tackle Box Guide to Common Saltwater Fishes of Southwest Florida*, written by Captain Ralph Allen and published through the Florida Sea Grant Program, is an excellent example of such a book.

## Fonts

Your book packager, typesetter or desk-top publishing program will have many standard fonts or typefaces available to use for the body text of your book. Use one that has serifs (the little hooks on each letter) rather than a sans serif font as those are easier to read:

**Century Schoolbook has serifs!**
**Arial does not!**

Sans serif fonts, like Arial, are good to use for chapter or section heads, cover design or advertising copy, but in text they can be tiresome to read. Try to avoid using them for the body of your book.

Make sure that type size fits your potential readership. Books for older eyes and for young children use a larger point size than those used for the average adult.

Type size is measured in points. Each point equals $\frac{1}{72}$ of an inch. Books commonly use type that is 10, 11, or maybe even 12 point. In this book we have used 11 point

New Caledonia for the body text. Over the length of a book, the font selection can make a considerable difference in the number of pages.

Here are some common book fonts. Notice the slight difference in the amount of space the same first three words used in these sample sentences:

This font is New Baskerville.
**This font is Garamond.**
**This font is Bookman.**
This font is Times New Roman.
This font is Palatino.

All of the above sample fonts are 11 point, but they will each result in a different length to your book.

The next examples of text, all in one font, show how the point size can affect the length and readability of a sentence. Be sure you select your font to fit your reader's age and eyesight .

This is Garamond 9 point.
This is Garamond 10 point.
**This is Garamond 11 point.**
**This is Garamond 12 point.**

As you can see the style of font and the point size can have an appreciable effect on the overall size of your book and its readability. If you are not working with a packager, study the fonts used in mainstream books so your choice will be appropriate to the type of book you are producing.

Remember that leading is important, too. Too much space between the lines of type, makes the eye lose contact while searching for the next line, and reading loses its flow. If the lines are too close together, they are hard to read. The leading used in this book is 14 point or about 127 percent of the point size of the typeface.

If you want to become more knowledgeable about typography and graphics, there are many good resources available. One such is *Adobe Magazine*, (formerly *Aldus Magazine*) published by the Adobe Corporation for the people who use its computer programs. Besides having an annual issue on typefaces, the magazine has frequent discussions of new type styles and writers offer practical advice on type design and typography.

In one issue[12], writer Robin Williams lists thirteen telltale signs of do-it-yourself desktop publishing. Just as the use of amateur covers, lack of credentials, the way you use type, indentations, underlining, caps, spacing after periods and gray boxes will expose your book as an amateur product. Williams concludes: "Creating professional-level type is simply a matter of becoming more aware of details. It doesn't take any more time to do it right, and these details are certainly not difficult to gain control over."

Her books, *Non-Designer's Design Book* and *A Blip in the Continuum* (both from Peachpit Press) share more secrets of typography and graphic design.

## Technology considerations

In what form will your packager want your manuscript?

So far we have talked about the many essential style elements of your book. The technology available to produce the guts of your book is also important. You need to be aware of the best and least expensive ways to get your manuscript to your packager.

If your manuscript is handwritten you will have no choice but to have it typed into a word-processing program that is compatible with your packager's page design and typesetting program. Retyping is time-consuming and costly, but it is the only alternative.

If you have typed your manuscript using a typewriter or older word processor, you may have two options for getting it translated into print.

The first, as with handwritten copy, is to have it retyped by hand into an your packager's program. This is usually the most labor-intensive and most costly option.

The second alternative is to have the pages scanned by an optical scanner with a good OCR (optical character recognition) program. Your packager or typesetter will have one in his armory of equipment. Scanning is less costly than retyping but works well only if your copy is extremely "clean." That means that if your ribbon is old, or if the keys of the typewriter need cleaning, your letter "o" may consistently be read by the scanner as an "a." This produces another of those technical problems that take time to fix, and time is money.

Scanning does not pick up handwritten notes or corrections, so if your manuscript is full of editorial corrections, you are probably still a candidate for a retype rather than a scan.

Scanning or typing costs can vary considerably, depending on where you have it done and what type of equipment is used.

For most serious writers, though, home computers and word processors are now more common than old-fashioned typewriters or a pencil and a legal pad.

Although computers make your work easier, sometimes they also can create headaches, especially for your packager. The use of obscure programs or old systems that are no longer compatible with modern standards will make the jobs of editing and typesetting more difficult.

You need to let your book packager know in what form your manuscript is coming, and, if on disk, what system and program was used. They will need to know whether the system is IBM compatible or Macintosh or a word processor. Most word processors, and many obsolete early computer systems such as Commodore and Kaypro, are not compatible with modern computers. Their technology has been passed by and forgotten by the modern computer industry.

Virtually any attempt by authors, however well-meaning, to format inside pages, will most likely end up being work that must be undone by editors and the typesetter. Try to resist the urge to try to make your draft look like a finished book. Just type the manuscript into your computer without fancy formats. All the time you spend making your work look "like a book" will confuse the program your work is going to be converted into. Then it will take more of his time because he or she will have to go through the files and delete all the formatting you put in.

The easier you make the job for the person you are hiring, the more you save on the project. If the programs are compatible, your book can be worked on by directly importing the text from your disk.

There are many good word processing programs that are easy to use, such as Word for Windows® from Microsoft, AmiPro®, WordPerfect®, and WordStar®.

These programs all have spellchecks, find-and-replace features, and block editing capabilities that make it easy for you to work with your copy. Keep in mind that spellcheck is no substitute for proofreading. For example, the spelling programs will recognize that "there," "they're," and "their" are all spelled correctly, but will not flag which is appropriate in the context of the sentence.

Another advantage of using a computer is that you can often hand your book to your packager on disk, rather than as a pile of hard copy.

Just as there is a big difference between printers and publishers, there is a big difference between ordinary word processing with a computer, and final page design and typesetting.

Many self-published books are produced by authors using word-processing programs. Unfortunately, despite the ability to use a good book typeface, their work may still end up looking less than professional without the page design and typesetting techniques that a quality packager can provide. For example, text needs to be balanced on pages. You need to avoid widows and orphans (the first or last words of a paragraph hanging alone at the top or bottom of a page or column). Letters need to be kerned (spaced aesthetically—fly is not kerned, fly is), and the leading must be adjusted. These are details for your professional book typesetter.

If you are generating your own camera-ready copy on a laser printer, make sure that the resolution is at least 600 dpi (dots per inch), preferably more. Most personal (home or office) laser printers, including those at quick print shops, produce only 300 dpi copy. Some of the newer laser printers will generate copy at 600 dpi. At lower resolutions the letters and graphics will not be as sharply defined and the finished product will not look as good as it should, especially to the practiced eyes of the wholesale buyers. If you are using a packager or are having your camera-ready generated by a service bureau, the resolution should be much higher to conform to industry standards. The camera-ready copy for this book was produced at 1200 dpi on a LaserMaster Unity 1200 LX-0 typesetter. Professional image setters produce copy at 2400 dpi.

According to Bob Lefebvre, founder of B&C Typesetting, "The formatting of a book is vastly different than that of any other printed product. Most desktop publishers shy away from this type of project due to their lack of knowledge concerning the anatomy of a book. Acceptable margins, text positioning, and the sequencing of sections are very precise elements. The professionalism of your finished product— your book—is all in the details."

## Submitting on disk

Some book manufacturers will accept your copy on disk and are able to do electronic prepress work. If you want to do this, be sure to work closely with your book manufacturer because there is still many subtle variations with computers and programs.

Unless you adhere to strict instructions about which files to include on your disk, and what format to have them in, there are no guarantees that what you see on your screen or on your draft copy will reproduce exactly the same on someone else's equipment.

The arguments for submitting on disk include possible cost savings, and getting a higher resolution output.

Some manufacturers can skip the camera-ready stage, going directly from disk to film or plate. Book manufacturers also tell us that going directly to film from disk will reduce or eliminate problems caused by toner on laser-printer-produced copy cracking, or even falling off the page.

# 5 Promoting your book

*Enthusiasm for books is what sells books.* — Fred Ciporen, publisher, *Publishers Weekly* [13]

WE HAVE SAID THIS before, but we can't emphasize it enough—a book is a product, and in addition to being professionally produced, it must be effectively promoted and marketed. Most products will not sell if they are not promoted. Your book will be best promoted through your own determination and diligent effort.

If you are the shy type (many of us started out that way) who absolutely freezes in public and would rather clean the cat box than greet the public, you better make sure you have a creative marketing program and money set aside to put into an advertising campaign. If you don't, you may end up with a garage full of wonderful books to leave to your heirs.

The point at which the delivery truck arrives at your door or storage unit may be the point at which you and your book packager part company, depending on your agreement. Some packagers have marketing services you can con-tract for once the production phase is completed. Others will guide you to marketing or publicity people. A few may even help you get launched as part of their deal with you. Discuss your arrangements with your packager well ahead of your delivery date so you can prepare your game plan. Remember, though, the ultimate success of marketing and sales will rest on your shoulders.

Keep in mind that market research is finding what customers want and filling their need, but

 You will want to get your marketing under way immediately to sell your book while it has a current copyright date. Something new is usually more interesting to the retail public that something that seems to be outdated.

you must have publicity to let the public know about what you have to sell them. Once you know who the most likely customers are for your book, then you have to let them know the book is available. You can "toot your own horn" any number of ways. Some methods cost money, but some don't. Make the most of the free ones!

## Reviews

There are two types of reviewers, each serving different categories of book buyers.

First there are those who review for the book trade. This group of reviewers includes *Publishers Weekly, Library Journal,* and *Kirkus Review,* among others. These publications are reviewing forthcoming books for those who

 Tampa poet Jorge Arteta self-published one thousand copies of his volume of poetry titled, *Welcome to Me, Myself...and I,* in November 1994. He used the services of a book packager so the book was properly credentialed and designed. Working tirelessly for his book, by June 1995 Jorge said he had sold almost eight hundred copies and had been honored by the Colombian Consulate in Chicago for his writing. One hundred guests, including the consul attended a reception in Arteta's honor, and most purchased autographed copies. He was approached about selling the foreign rights to his book. His readers are already asking him to do a second volume. Jorge did not wait to be discovered, he went after success and found it on his own.

own and manage bookstores and libraries, and for the wholesalers and distributors.

The second category are those who review for the retail consumer—those folks who will go to the bookstore and buy the books. These reviewers include the major newspapers, such as the *New York Times,* many specialty magazines, such as automotive or entertainment, and local or national media.

You will need to decide well before your book is released if you want to try to be reviewed nationally. If so, you will need to have bound galleys (sometimes called "Cranes" after the company that first printed them) made to submit to reviewers who require them. Bound galleys are made from a set of your page proofs and are often bound with an inexpensive cardstock printed cover.

The cover of a bound galley is different than the cover of the final book. It should specify the title, author, author's biographical information, your publication date, price, ISBN, number of pages and illustrations, first printing figures, and your anticipated advertising and promotion budget, plus rights sale information.

Those who review for the trade generally want the bound galleys or even a copy of the page proofs at least three to four months before the planned publication date. That way, book buyers can read the review and order the book so as to have it in stock on the publication date and thereby take advantage of the marketing hype.

Those who review for the consumer are not always as concerned with the time frame of the review. They will want to see the finished product just before, or at least shortly after, the release date. Sometimes they will accept an advance reader edition, which is substantively complete.

Remember that there are thousands of new books published each year and, although only a small percentage are submitted for review, your book will need to stand out to be considered. *Publishers Weekly* alone receives six hundred titles a week for consideration in its *Library Journal*.

Call the editors of the publications to determine current policies for reviews. Do not be discouraged if larger papers don't have space for reviews. Local books are competing for review space with the national best-sellers, and many book-page editors find it's less

 According to an article by Ellen Graham in the June 28, 1995 edition of the *Wall Street Journal,* romance novels are finally being reviewed by mainstream publications. The romance category of books is estimated by some sources as a $1 billion business but even best-sellers have been ignored by reviewers until recently. Graham wrote, "As more romance titles appear in hardcover and hit national best-seller lists, the books are harder to dismiss."

problematic for them to critique the "safe" books—the ones which have already been reviewed by other sources—than to chance an unknown. Reviewers at medium-sized papers (a circulation of less than 200,000) receive as many as one hundred books a week—

unsolicited—from large and small presses. The homemade looking books are quickly put aside. One book reviewer told us that because she believes that cookbooks will be more likely to be discussed in the life-style section, and religious books may catch the eye of the religion editor, she limits her consideration to books of very general interest. And then she is further guided by national book promotion.

You may send bound galleys to *Publishers Weekly, Literary Marketplace, Library Journal, Kirkus Review, New York Times Book Review,* and the *ALA Booklist.*

A review by any of these major trade publications can be extremely beneficial. *Booklist,* for instance, is a guide to current print

Author Tom Grimshaw's *In Like a Lamb...Out Like a Lion* has received excellent reviews from magazines which cover car racing. In May 1995, the book's account of the incredible driving career of John Buffum, America's most famous rally race car driver was reviewed by Andrew Bornhop, in *Road and Track Magazine.* Grimshaw, a gifted writer, served as Buffum's codriver throughout the peak of his career, giving him special biographical insight. The reviews in magazines which cater to a specific audience have produced orders from bookstores and readers around the country.

and non-print materials considered worthy of purchase by small and medium-sized public libraries and school library media centers. A review in *Booklist* constitutes a recommendation for purchase by libraries, according to the American Library Association.

Target your review sources very carefully rather than randomly sending out copies. You might even contact the reviewers first to determine if they are interested in seeing your book.

Even if a paper or magazine does not have a book review section, you can often interest an appropriate editor or writer (business, medical, sports, religion, or features) in writing about you and your book. Some of the best press coverage for books we have seen is through feature writers.

And, don't forget about radio or television reviews. Millions of people listen to "Fresh Air" each day on National Public Radio. "Morning Edition" also reviews

Smart Self-Publishing

Write your own review of the book, (or ask someone with a credible title to write one for you) to enclose with your review copy. Your succinct review, hitting the salient points of the book, may pique the interest of the reviewer and at least make the job easier.

 Speaking of giving away copies of your book, you will discover that many people you know (and some you don't) will have their hands out for a free copy. Sometimes they are very brazen. Make a list of the people you want to give a copy to, and set some aside for legitimate reviews. Then, be ready to tell all your "new best friends" that publishing is a business and your book is a product. They either can purchase the book at the bookstore, or from you—perhaps at a special discount price.

books, as does "All Things Considered." You might also send your book to national weekly news magazines such as *U.S. News & World Report, Time,* and *Newsweek* and even the Sunday newspaper supplement, *Parade* magazine.

There are also opportunities for book reviews in many specialty magazines and professional journals. If you have a religious topic, you might look toward church newsletters for advertising or as a source of reviews.

Depending on your subject and the professionalism of your product, you might be fortunate enough to attract national attention. Realistically, though, don't expect to be reviewed by the traditional media sources like the "Big Guys" and don't pin your marketing plans on reviews. The giant publishing houses are sinking hundreds of thousands of dollars into media campaigns, even to the extent of "buying" the covers of major trade magazines as advertisements to catch the attention of reviewers and bookstores. (See page 23.) The hype works, and often the books sell, no matter how poor the quality of the material.

We also strongly suggest concentrating your effort locally, or at least begin in an area with a radius of no more than a half-day drive from your home, and taking advantage of all available publicity.

If your book does not get reviewed, you might call the reviewers and find out why your book wasn't reviewed. Listen carefully to the answer so that you will learn from their advice.

## Writing press releases that work

There are two people to keep in mind when you are writing your press release. The first is the person at the newspaper (radio station, magazine, television station) who will read it and decide whether, when and how it will be used. The second is the reader or listener you ultimately want to reach.

Here are some essentials:

✓ Use publisher letterhead, and include your address, phone number, fax number and E-mail address, if you have them.

✓ Offer to send a review copy if the reviewer wants one.

✓ Include the date you sent the release or when it can be used.

✓ Emphasize what is unique about the book and author's credentials in the subject or ties to the area.

✓ Tailor your basic press release to a given market by changing the first paragraph or two.

✓ Focus your release on what makes the information newsworthy.

✓ Keep the length of your press release to a page if possible.

✓ Include the title and subtitle of your book as well as pertinent information: publisher, price, number of pages, ordering information, and number of photographs.

✓ Think about the selling points of your book. Why should newspaper readers, want to buy it? Will it help them solve a problem or make them rich?

✓ Decide if focusing on the author is a selling point. That isn't always the case. If the author is an expert in the field or has wide name recognition, capitalize on that.

Some hometown papers will use a release just because the author is local, but many papers in larger metropolitan editions need more reason to include even a brief mention in a book section. Keep in mind that the book is a product and you must make consumers want to buy it. What are the book's features and benefits?

There are some PR companies such as Publishers News Service

 Put all your important information in the first two or three paragraphs of your press release.

(See Appendix B.) that will write and distribute camera-ready, feature-length newspaper articles and fillers about nonfiction titles to newspapers around the country. Many smaller or weekly papers will simply paste the prefab article directly on their page. If you are not good at writing short articles, this may be an avenue to explore.

Newspaper staff edits articles, stories, and press releases to fit the available space. As you write your release or article, study it from this point of view: If an editor cuts my release, will the essential facts still be included?

Don't expect editors or news clerks to spend time rewriting your release. You will have a much better chance of having your material used if you do it right. If you send out a longer press

*Here's an example of how to pack information into a press release:*

---

(Publisher letterhead)

### New book reveals the words of a loving God

(date of release)
(person to contact and phone number)

Virginia Testa, of Englewood, Florida, was at a low point in her life when she was called by God to write His words to a broken, lost and suffering people. She was surprised and overwhelmed, but accepted God's call, and the result is a new book: *The Mystique of God, as revealed through the Holy Spirit to Virginia Testa.* Mrs. Testa will sign copies from (time) on (date) at (name and address of store or location of signing).

The 96-page book, priced at $12.95, "gives new hope, comfort and joy to hurting people," said Evangelist Terry Radcliff. "You will sense God's great love for his children illuminated through each page. These prophetic revelations of the Holy Spirit give insight to the heart and mind of God."

Mrs. Testa had never expected to be a writer. Born in Brooklyn, N.Y., she became a certified professional secretary and was employed as such by Exxon until her retirement in 1984. Those who read *The Mystique of God* are touched by its message and authenticity. The book's publication is especially timely because secular bookstores are finding a great interest in religious and prophetic books as the turn of the century draws near.

For review copies and interviews call (name and phone number).

-30-

---

release, you may include more information on the author (always write about yourself in the third person) and more details from the book. But you can see in the sample release, we have included the news "peg" (the booksigning—including the who, what, why, when, and where), a little of what the book is about, its cost, its cover and where to get more information about it. You should put the name of your book or publishing house and a page number in one of the upper corners, especially if the pages of the release are not stapled. At the bottom of the first page, and each subsequent page

If your book jacket or cover is designed correctly, you can recycle that information into your advertisements and press releases.

except the last, write the word "more" in parenthesis. The "-30-" or "###" symbol is code that tells editors they have reached the end of your release and haven't lost a page on their desk.

File your press releases in the memory of your computer or word processor so that you can quickly retrieve and modify them to reflect critical reviews, new booksignings, or awards or to modify them for a specific audience.

If your book is more readily available through you or a fulfillment house than it is through a bookstore, include the cost of shipping and sales tax, plus an address or the 800 number of your fulfillment house in your release.

In the section on newspapers, we have included more about how to write and modify press releases.

## Booksignings

Most authors plan on using book-signings as a major way to publicize and sell their books. Some book-stores enjoy hosting these events, others don't. Some store managers tell us one reason they don't host signings is that they don't want an author to feel disappointed if only a few people show up.

The first rule of booksignings is to hope for sales, but do not be disappointed if you don't have many. If you have a good product, the store will generally buy extra

Don't schedule booksignings or other promotional events until you have the books in hand! Many an author has had to back out of a signing commitment because of a printing delay or delivery problem. It is not only an embarrassing situation, but valuable publicity is lost.

copies to display before and after your visit so that customers who could not attend can buy at another time. Sign the extra copies while you are there so the store can use shelf advertisers for "autographed copies."

Send out your press releases at least two weeks before the event. Put good quality fliers on every bulletin board in town. If you have access to a laser printer, create a flier or small poster on colorful bond paper, using large type and an easy-to-read font.

In addition to giving copies of the poster to the store to display, see if motels and time-shares will let you post it. Look for community bulletin boards outside supermarkets and laundromats.

Print smaller announcements for the store to give to every customer or to stuff in bags during the week prior to the signing.

Offer to split the cost of advertising and refreshments with the store. Some large stores may have a marketing department, but as a rule, don't count on the store to provide your publicity. Many of the superstores have monthly or weekly calendars that they print and distribute.

Try to make an "event" out of your booksigning. Dot Bowles, regional manager for Books-A-Million, says that if you have

---

## Great holiday gift!

Jerrell Shofner to autograph his award-winning new book: A History of Altamonte Springs

Here on Friday, (date) 2-4 P.M.

---

written a cookbook or gardening book or other how-to-do-it book, have a demonstration. Have music or a history display in conjunction with your booksigning to help attract customers and interest. Brainstorm with the bookstore manager for ways to build interest in you and your book.

Usually the store will provide a table and chair, but to be sure, ask. If the store has a sound system, ask them to announce your signing or event before and during your allotted time.

Take plenty of copies of your book with you. You want your table to be full of them. Typically, the store handles the sales while you do the signing. Find out from the manager on duty if the books are to be paid for before you sign them. If they are, don't sign a book unless you are first shown a sales receipt by the customer.

Ask each customer how to spell the name of the person to whom the book will be signed. Write the name on a pad, and/or spell it back before making the inscription in the book. You'd be surprised by the variations in the spelling of names, and if you spell it wrong, you have probably wasted a copy of your book. If you do goof, save the book to use as a review copy.

To save time trying to think of something different to write for each customer, develop a standard greeting unless someone asks for special wording.

Talk about your book and your subject constantly. Visit with customers even if they don't buy your book at the time. You might make the sale later, and the customers talking about your book to their friends might publicize the book through word of mouth.

You may feel a bit like the barker at a carnival, but it's better to talk to people and give them a reason to look at your product rather than just letting them pass by. Stand up and greet your potential customers. You should sit down only to sign books or maybe to take a quick break when no one is in the store. Don't catch up on your reading during the booksigning, don't act bored and don't let one or two customers monopolize your time.

*Radio and TV star, Durward Kirby, center, and his wife, "Pax," are joined by their friend, Willard Scott, at a booksigning at MacIntosh Bookshop, Sanibel Island, Florida. More than sixty fans waiting in line enjoyed the banter between Scott and the Kirbys.*

Provide printed hanging cards for your books on the store shelves that say: AUTOGRAPHED COPY.

 Keep copies of your book in your car. If the store you stop at *doesn't* stock your book, you may be able to make a sale on the spot. This works especially well in an independently owned store, especially in high traffic areas.

Be polite but keep yourself available for the next customer.

Do "drive-by" booksignings. Drop in at bookstores that have your book in stock just to sign copies. In fact, if you have books in your car, stop at any independent and offer to do a signing on the spot. The store might go for it and you would have a new outlet as well as good PR. Many readers believe that there is value in purchasing an autographed copy of a book. By making unannounced visits to bookstores, you may actually stimulate sales and interest in your book. Joan Simonds, owner of the Island Book Nook in Sanibel, Florida, finds that author visits remind her to restock and may stimulate sales while the author is in the store.

You will find many opportunities to sell your book, but the key is to select those where you have the best opportunity to reach your public. You may be able to get a table at a book fair, flea market, church bazaar or a trade show either free or very reasonably. If there is a fee, you might join with other authors and spread the cost. Add in your transportation and other expenses, the cost of handouts, and time away from other projects to see if the exposure is worthwhile. Sometimes it is; sometimes not. But these affairs offer visibility and give authors an opportunity to network.

If you are having a book sale and signing at a festival, craft fair, or a flea market, or maybe as part of a seminar, make sure you take your own table, chair, books, promotional materials, your receipt book, and a money bag or box with a variety of change. Out of doors you might also want a beach umbrella, a cooler with water or soda, and perhaps even a cell phone.

**Television and radio interviews**

Self-publishing authors usually have invested most of their available resources in the production of their book, and often there isn't much money left over. Radio and television advertising campaigns are expensive. Simple television commercials, even if they are produced by a local company, may cost more than $1,000 to shoot, and more than $100 each time they are aired on local network stations.

If you really think a commercial will help sell your book, try the local cable channels where air time is usually more affordable. Sometimes "packages" are available that will lower the cost of each spot if you buy in quantity. But as with most advertising, you need to show the spot fairly frequently to have it register.

Experts say it usually takes at least three times for viewers to remember or pay attention to what they are seeing or hearing on the tube. Think about your own listening and tune-out habits.

 One of our regional TV channels, a network affiliate, had a feature called "Made in Southwest Florida," which appeared once a week on the 6:00 P.M. news. We called the station to ask if books could be considered something made in Southwest Florida because indeed the author, illustrator and the printer fit the demographics. Bingo! A reporter and camera crew were sent to the house, where they filmed the illustrator at work, and the author at the computer. We had five minutes of free publicity on television! Heady with success, we then talked our way onto the same station's noon news and talk show. The publicity helped us place our books in area bookstores.

Radio time can also be expensive, although usually less so than television. You may be able to get some free publicity for your booksigning by writing up the details for the local radio station or local announcement cable television announcement channel, often called something like "Community Bulletin Board." They usually need the information ten days to two weeks in advance of the event, so don't wait until the last minute.

## Talk shows

The best publicity in life is often free. Get on talk shows. One way to get their attention is by advertising in *Radio and Television Interview Report*. Some talk show hosts charge for interviews so ask up front if there is a fee and if so, what the fees are.

This publication consists of quarter-, half-, and full-page display ads that authors and others place to make the industry aware of their books and their willingness to be a guest. It is sent to virtually every talk show producer in the country—and it works.

Or, purchase Joe Sabah's kit for a list of talk show hosts around the nation that are looking for guests every day, and information about how reach them. (Lists of media specialists are in Appendix B.)

You can also telephone television and radio stations and talk to the person who books the guests. Give them a good reason to have you on the show. Be bold and creative. Remember, your "audition" is your telephone conversation with them. If you don't seem to have a lively personality and a good phone voice they probably will not invite you.

Talk show hosts are busy and often have several authors on their shows in a week's time. They find it impossible to read all the books that the authors submit. So to save them and yourself embarrassment:

✓ Write a list of questions you would like to be asked and get it, along with a review copy and biographical data and information about you, your book and its topic, to the station ahead of time. If the interview is to be in person, bring another copy with you so that you have something to refer to.

✓ Before your interview, ask if you may mention the 800 number of your fulfillment house or distributor so that callers may immediately order the book. If your host agrees, be sure to mention the number frequently. Sometimes the host will ask you, "Where can people get your book?" as a handy lead-in.

✓ If you are a guest on a television program, hold up your book now and then for a few moments as you talk so that the cover is visible. Keep the book tipped slightly toward the table so the lights won't be reflected into the camera lens. Better yet, get the host to do it in a way that will insure a close-up.

✓ Keep your discussion lively and entertaining. Find out in advance what the audience is like so that you can talk to the listeners on their own level.

✓ Make sure the receptionist at the station has information about how to order your book in case there are calls after the show is over.

✓ Many radio talk shows can be "patched," or transmitted by phone right from the comfort of your own home. Joe Sabah suggests that to set the mood, dress as though you were on the show in person, and stand up during the interview as though you were speaking to a live audience. It will do wonders for your presentation.

Ted Nicholas, one of the gurus of promotion and self-publishing, has said that selling books is very much like a candidate running for president. The candidate counts votes one at a time, and books are sold copy by copy.

 Ask about the policies of the paper concerning using your photograph, or a copy of the book's cover so that you know what to include with your press release. Sometimes a newspaper will use a photograph you provide; others take their own.

## Newspapers

A basic assumption of this book is that you will try to sell as many books as possible in your own community, where people that you know, and who know you, live. That's also where you know, or can get to know, the booksellers and the media folks. You also need to know who does what at the newspaper, and what the special section deadlines are. Ask how much lead time the editor needs if you want the information in the paper's calendar of events, announcement section, or in the booksigning section (the Sunday editions of some papers have them). And you need to ask who should get a copy of the press release since different people may be assigned to each of those details. Also ask about reviews and features.

 Stamp your review copies: COMPLIMENTARY COPY. NOT FOR RESALE.

In general, you want to make sure that if you part with a review copy of your book, it really will be reviewed. Not all papers do reviews, but often you can get a nice feature story about your book and yourself in those that don't, especially if you are able to emphasize a local angle.

Once you have been publicized, readers will begin to ask for your book at the bookstore or the library, and that is the name of the game. In your press releases, publicize the names of the retail outlets where your book may be available and the phone number for your distributor or fulfillment house.

Keep in mind that in the overall scheme of things at a daily paper, a press release about the publication of a new book or a booksigning is very seldom the top story of the day. Try to tie your release into an event that is worthy of a news announcement to give the media a reason to use it. Be patient if your story or press release doesn't appear immediately. But, if several weeks go by and you still haven't seen the story, there is nothing wrong with calling to find out if the press release was received, or if the writer or reporter needs additional information to complete the story. If you have a fax machine—wonderful for distributing press releases—send another copy. Be sure to direct it to the specific person or desk, such as religion, food, sports, or features, that will deal with the information. Include the name and phone number of someone who may be contacted for more information, and that person's title (author, publisher).

When we developed the basic information announcing the release of *TeleVisionaries*, we made it a point to customize the lead (first sentence) to whichever part of the country it was being sent and made sure it promoted Jim Robertson's own experience at the television stations in that area. The author information was a selling point in this instance because of his role as a founder of public television stations in several cities.

 Author Jack Alexander had been working for two years on the history of a unique land development in Southwest Florida—a story of unfulfilled developer promises that led to on-going lawsuits and a steady series of owner-managers. Rotonda West was also the site of ABC-TV's "Superstars" series during the 1970s where sports champions competed against each other in their areas of nonexpertise. Just as the book, *Rotonda: The Vision and the Reality* was being prepared for the editing and production, two major events put the book in the heart of news: O. J. Simpson, who had been one of the superstars on the show, was arrested for murder. Secondly, Rotonda was again for sale. The author was able to capitalize on the Simpson connection and news about the sale in the advance publicity for the book.

That led to a two-page spread about Rotonda by Tom Matrullo in the "Business Monday" section of the *Sarasota Herald-Tribune,* featuring the book with a photograph of the author.

No matter how good or bad a review or story, always send a personal thank-you note to the reviewer, writer or interviewer

## Negative press

To a point, bad press and negative reviews are better than none at all. People may not remember the details of an article, but they may well remember the title or topic and buy the book. Most books banned in Boston have enjoyed good sales—even, perhaps especially, in Boston. If you have produced a quality product, you will avoid reviewers criticism of editing, production, and documentation. Instead, they will write a discussion of the material.

Don't chew out the newspaper writers or reviewers if you disagree with their point of view. It's OK to ask for a correction (please, not a "retraction") if there is a glaring factual error such as your phone number. If the errors are minor, just suggest pleasantly, "In future reference, please correct the following information:...."

It is astonishing how wrong information, such as the book's title or your name, can appear in print, even when a reporter or clerk has correct material in front of them. It's best to phrase your

 You can learn a lot about advertising by studying professional national ads in major newspapers and magazines, and direct-mail pieces that grab your attention. Or attend a marketing seminar. There are also many good books on the subject in your local bookstore.

request for corrections nicely. You do *not* want to make enemies of the media. You may need them later to publicize your signings or other newsworthy events.

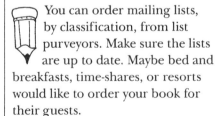 Have lots of extra covers or dust jackets printed during the book's production, then print your flier on the other side. You can have the printer switch from coverstock to a cheaper, lighter-weight paper for use in mailings. Write a catchy headline that grabs the readers' attention and provides a reason for them to buy your book.

You can order mailing lists, by classification, from list purveyors. Make sure the lists are up to date. Maybe bed and breakfasts, time-shares, or resorts would like to order your book for their guests.

**Smart Self-Publishing**

## Advertising that works

If you decide you want to place some print ads, make sure they are in the magazines or newspapers that your specific readers read. For example, if you have written about World War II, consider advertising in veterans' magazines. If you have written a book of poetry, perhaps advertise it in a literary magazine. An advertisement in a specialty magazine may lead to a review of your book in that magazine—or in one of its competitors.

Advertising is expensive, and certainly you can't afford to advertise in every magazine or directory. Be selective in your choices and make your ads work for you. Some advertising publications will allow you to have "free editorial" space if you purchase an ad. You might be able to write a regular column, if the publication reaches your target audience, for the price of an ad.

For example, advertising book. Try including different coupons or "special offers" so you can track the effectiveness of your ads in various media. The replies you receive should become the basis for a mailing list. However, if you are giving your message to the wrong market, you may receive hundreds of replies asking for free information—but no actual sales. Advertising packaging services for self-publishing authors in a magazine which caters to writers who seek a publisher to buy their book is targeting the wrong market.

Including a testimonial or quote about your book or the topic is often compelling. For advertising purposes, put your selling point in quotes: "Congratulations on your success with *Smart Self-Publishing*. A lot of books come out on this topic, and yours seems to have joined the select few that are widely considered to be musts for the professional libraries of new publishers." Steve Carlson, *Big Books From Small Presses*.

Avoid having a headline in your ad that asks a question that can be answered, "No." You will be giving your customer an excuse for not buying your book.

## Best-seller lists

As you are developing your strategy, it's important to be aware of the odds of making a splash, at least initially, in the national market. In short, without well-funded marketing and publicity, it is virtually impossible. The *Wall Street Journal* (September 7, 1995) explained how the best-seller lists work. Some lists are generated by sales from chain stores, others may take into consideration sales from independents, or drugstore or supermarket distribution.

*WSJ* staff reporter Patrick M. Reilly noted, "[The] fact is that best-seller lists are ... subject to the whims of those who compile them, and worst of all, in some cases easy for authors and publishers to manipulate." He added that making the list may determine how the book is promoted in a store or on a shelf. The lists may not include mega-sales through book clubs, or categories of books such as Christian or romance. Making the list is no guarantee that the book is well-written or has merit, but simply that it's marketing program has been successful.

### Direct mail

Many self-publishing authors are selling successfully using direct marketing. You can develop your own short list from your holiday card list, friends, relatives, business associates, local clubs and organizations, college friends— anyone you think might order your book. For added incentive, offer them a pre-publication or multiple-copy discount.

Betsy Lampé of Rainbow Books has a great illustration of how targeted direct marketing works successfully. After publishing *An Ounce of Preservation: A Guide to the Care of Papers and Photographs,* by Craig A. Tuttle, Lampé did a mailing to genealogical societies and other groups and organizations that have an interest in preserving paper. The initial data base included 10,000 listings. Lampé says that direct mailing from her very focused list has resulted in a sales response of between 20 and 60 percent.

"By the time we do the revised and expanded second edition in 1997, we will have gone through at least ten print runs [of 2,000 to 4,000 each]," Lampé says. The direct mail is in addition to having Tuttle appear regularly on television talk shows and the Discovery Channel's *Home Matters.* Lampé primarily focuses on nonbookstore markets for sales.

### Bulk mailings

For bulk mailings of fliers and other promotional materials, try to find a business or an organization that has a bulk-mail permit you can use. Better yet, find one that has a permit to use "precanceled" stamps. Having a stamp, even a bulk-mail, precanceled stamp, on your mailing makes it appear more personal than simply having a preprinted imprint and permit number. For bulk mail, you must have a minimum of two hundred pieces. All must be the same size and weight, must have the same contents, and may not include anything handwritten except your signature. With the precanceled stamp program, you are not as rigidly controlled. It is still necessary to have a minimum of two hundred pieces, but within limits they can vary in size, weight, and content. You still can't have any personal messages, but it is OK to have computer-generated mail-merge. See your postal service bulk-mail facility for details.

## Speakers bureaus

Depending on your subject matter and your public speaking ability, you may be able to promote your book through a speakers bureau.

 Tag and Judi Powell, owners of Top of the Mountain Publishing in Tampa, Florida, are effective promoters of their business. They market their books in an extensive catalog, and they travel to Europe to sell foreign rights, often selling the same book several times over (to different buyers) for translation into different languages. They also combine books with tapes to create successful packages which they market at their seminars, in their catalogs, at trade shows and during their media appearances. Tag and Judi rarely let any opportunity slip by to promote their products.

Aside from national celebrities, the bureaus also feature authors on many subjects such as health, motivation, business and sports.

Mike Frank, author of *For Professional Speakers Only* and founder of Speakers Unlimited, says that it is vital for authors who are considering the speaking circuit to develop a "bureau friendly" demo tape from ten minutes to an hour in length. Bureau friendly means you should not include references to your address or your telephone number in your video or on your brochure. If you are accepted as a client, all bookings must be made by the bureau so as to avoid confusion.

Also, Frank says, you must indicate your expected fee and other requirements. His book explains how to create the demo tape, and is, itself, an example of how an author has filled a specific niche by putting information in book form, then selling the copies himself at full price.

## Using the Internet

Although the information super-highway is not yet easily affordable in all parts of the country, you may want to think about advertising or communicating with others about your book on the Internet or the World Wide Web. Some book distributors, bookstores, authors, publishers and even publisher's organizations, such as the Florida Publishers Association are advertising on the Web. We hesitate to be too enthusiastic because as yet there are no hard results by which to judge the effectiveness of those ads. Many of the Web sites register

Author Linda Salisbury was fortunate to have her friend, Mary Williams, a well-known social columnist for the *Charlotte/AM,* offer to dress as a tomato at an early booksigning for *Good-bye Tomato, Hello Florida.* The "tomato" did a terrific job, and attracted buyers who might not have come otherwise. She was also willing to make later public appearances in behalf of the book, including riding on a float for the book in a chamber of commerce parade.

many "hits," but so far, overall, the sales are minimal. Some authors report good results from having their book advertised on their Web home pages, others are still waiting for traffic on the information super highway to come their way.

Our general advice is to be aware of the tremendous marketing potential of the Web, and try to position yourself to become a part of it, if affordable provider services are available and it suits your needs. (See Appendix D for more information about Web pages.)

## Miscellaneous attention-grabbers

When you are presenting a program, or having an autograph session, make use of all the space around you.

✓ Invest in a sturdy easel and some stiff posterboard, then make attractive displays about yourself and your book. Include copies of any reviews or features written about you or your work.

✓ Have the cover of your book photographed and enlarged to poster size at a photography or discount store such as a pharmacy. Get poster frames from a discount store and you will have a dramatic graphic to catch the attention of passersby or for a window display.

✓ Make magnetic signs for your car. For less than fifty dollars, your vehicle will become a billboard for your book whether you are on the road or parked in town. We have actually sold books to fellow travelers who notice the magnetic signs at gas stations. Keep your message simple, such as: Author of *Whizzle While You Work* (and either your 800 or home phone number). After we recom-

 We first heard about readers theater when contacted by librarian Helen Burns. Helen and her librarian partner, Lee Buckner, wanted permission to adapt Linda's books for their Books Alive! programs. They had developed a special presentation to coincide with Linda's talk at a fund-raising luncheon for the library. The librarians had been performing sketches at retirement centers, churches, community organizations, libraries, parks, and at shopping malls. "Have sketches, will travel," became their motto. Since then, they have done several radio presentations, and have invited Linda to be on talk shows with them to discuss her books.

To better your chances of promoting sales to bookstores and libraries:

✓Produce your own promotional book review for librarians to use.

✓Have a banner made with your publishing company's name or book's title on it that you can display at booksignings and book fairs.

✓Print bookmarks to include with every book sale.

✓Have someone read your book on tape for sale or gifts.

✓Get your publishing name in programs, such as theater, sports, or symphony as a sponsor or advertiser.

✓Donate some copies of your book to be given away on talk shows, chamber of commerce open houses or fund raisers on public television or radio.

✓Give a copy of your book to your public radio's reading service to be read on the air to the blind.

✓Join with other authors to cooperatively rent and share time at a flea market booth or to host a table at a festival. Split the cost of advertising in catalogs.

✓Make your booksignings into events.

✓Let a good friend plan a special party in your honor (or you plan it yourself) when your book is released. Invitations should be clear that the author will be selling autographed copies of the book and what the price is.

mended the use of magnetic signs to one of our authors, he told us he had sold three books within the first week of using them on his car. Those were only the sales he knew of; there may have been others.

✓Have a friend dress up in a costume relevant to your book. In trade jargon, that person is called a "walk-around." Send your walk-around through the mall with a copy of your book to attract attention and direct people to your signing. Sometimes off-premise advertising by mall stores is not allowed, so be sure to get approval from the mall management first. Obviously some books lend themselves better than others to this approach.

✓Ask your local bookstore to save extra "dumps" for you, or you can order them from speciality companies. Dumps are the cardboard displays in which large publishing houses often ship their books. They hope that the ready-made displays will get floor or counter space in the store so their books will be showcased. Bookstores don't have the room for all those floor displays and throw away most of the dumps. Pick through what they save for you and keep the ones that fit your book for your own displays at trade shows or book-signings. You will have to create your own advertising to paste over what has been preprinted.

✓ Have your publishing imprint stitched on shirts and caps to identify you in public.
✓ Have a banner or table drape made with your logo for book fairs and booth displays.

## Readers theater and library cards

A delightful and unusual way to have your book promoted is readers theater, a simple production which enlivens and demonstrates your product. We've heard librarians call it a "trailer" for your book.

Helen Burns and Lee Buckner of the Books Alive! Readers Theater Troupe describe the concept as follows:

"In readers theater, you use the author's words with a few props, body language and subtle and creative use of your voice the way an artist uses a palette to present scenes of such color and simplicity that the viewer is drawn in from the very first word. Without props, scenery, and stage action, imagination creates the character, the emotion, and the scene. Using the full dramatic possibilities inherent in reading aloud, the performers share the characters' experiences. The tale is further supported and embraced by the reader's inflection and projection, emphasis and body language."

Librarians do readers theater; theatrical groups do it. So do colleges and churches. Readers theater accepts material that is easily adapted to presentation with minimal props and setting. Parts of novels, diaries, plays, newspaper columns, essays, poems, and biographies can be developed into scripts for one or more persons.

During a performance, Helen and Lee use about five segments from Linda's book (or those by other authors). They assume different roles simply by changing a hat or other prop, as they "act out" the selected passages. Lee Buckner said that readers theater is a tremendous marketing tool. After a performance audience members always want to locate copies for purchase, and will indignantly call the library if the bookstore is out of copies.

Books Alive! (and Linda) received special publicity before and after one performance when the dialogue from Linda's books were "signed" for the deaf during a presentation at a regional mall.

Librarians may also write short book reviews for various editions of a regional newspaper. The reviews feature newly received books of particular interest at county libraries. Reviews are also produced for newsletters of local organizations.

Many library support organizations host fund-raisers such as book fairs and luncheons at which local authors are invited to speak and sell their books. We recommend you give a dollar or more per book sold back to the organization. You will get a tax write-off and will probably be asked back, too.

Ruth Adele Mysel was honored at an elegant champagne brunch given by her friends when her book, *Circle of Love*, a love story in poetry and sculpture, came off the press. As an added touch, the author's sculptures were on display as part of the table's centerpiece. Mysel, a multi-talented artist also signed her books at gallery showings and gave talks about her photographs, sculptures and other art forms. She would wear bright clothing and a hat to draw attention to herself.

Author Myrtle Kennerly, at age ninety three, published a book of her memories including meeting

*Poet Ruth Adele Mysel, dressed to the nines in her trademark red, white and blue, signs her book,* Circle of Love, *at Kingsley's Book Emporium in Sarasota, Florida.*

former president Theodore Roosevelt in 1914, when they were both passengers aboard the first boat to traverse the Panama Canal. During the Depression she and her husband sold eggs and, for a while, even were bootleggers.

Later they bought a boarding house in Baltimore and, over the years, she became "mother" to hundreds of students from the Peabody Conservatory.

The perfect touch for her first autograph party, which was held at

*"Ben," the alien , with two eager children at a booksigning of* Dino-man, The Untold Story, *at Books-A-Million in Port Charlotte, Florida.*

a gallery, was a cello trio playing classical music.

One of the most extraordinary efforts we have observed is Brofam Books' promotion of *Dino-Man: The Untold Story* by James Brotherton. To sell the action-adventure book involving dinosaurs, aliens and people from several centuries, this family-owned company had cover artist, Chris Pearl, create the image of a central character, Ben, an alien. Ben's face first appeared on T-shirts for a local senior league softball team. Every time the team won (and they became state champions), the book's title, *Dino-Man*, was in the sports headlines. That captivated the interest of sports columnists, especially when Brofam challenged the Media All-Stars to softball game in a stadium as a part of a large community event. (Dino-Man won.) By the time Brofam was ready for its first book signing at Books-A-Million, clerks were wearing the Dino-Man T-shirt, the author came through a smoky, simulated time tunnel in the parking lot while a local radio station did a live broadcast. Children couldn't wait to touch, hug and be photographed with the walk-around character of Ben, who had been professionally fashioned by an art studio. Brofam offered free barbecued "Dino-ribs" and cookies, and free four-color bookmarks featuring Ben's face. Working with a local promoter, the time tunnel, walk-around and booksigning was immediately booked for a number of grand openings of businesses, and the activities will be repeated at other book stores in the region.

Although not every book lends itself to such an event, nor can every publishing house afford to design and purchase posters, bookmarks and other items to sell or give away, Brofam illustrates a very basic principal: Enthusiasm sells books. The Brotherton family (Brofam) is making the most of every opportunity to promote and sell *Dino-Man*.

*Author Bill Gorvine with Betsy Lampé in front of the Florida Publishers Booth at the 1996 Southeast Booksellers Association trade show in Nashville. Bill and and his wife, Enid, "worked the floor" to promote his new book,* Rekindling Your Spirit: Messages to Live By.

# 6 Business details

*Getting myself set up to sell my books had an added benefit. It gave me an unexpected chance to promote my book with people such as the clerk at the sales tax office.* —Virginia Testa, author of *The Mystique of God.*

THERE IS A LOT MORE to becoming a publishing company—even a *self-publishing* company—than simply deciding to publish your book.

Becoming a publisher is really becoming a business. Although you should have your basic business plan formulated before you begin, you will need to work on the technical aspects of becoming a publisher with your book packager and/or your accountant while your book is being produced.

One of the first things you will need to do is select a name and design a letterhead and/or logo. Then, unless you are going to use an ISBN supplied by your packager, you will have to apply for a bank of ISBNs as outlined in chapter four in the section about credentials. Your packager should be able to obtain all publishing credentials for your book for you or will advise you as to how to do the leg work yourself.

You will also have to establish your business formally, that is, register your business or "fictitious" name with the proper governmental authority.

In our area we needed to register with our county zoning department. To do that, we had stationery made with our company name and address on which we wrote the cover letter that accompanied our application. We were able to create the initial letterhead with our desktop publishing program. Notice of the application was then published, at our expense, in the legal-notices section of one of the local newspapers. When no objections were received, and our type of business reviewed by the zoning department to make sure that we were in compliance with local zoning codes, we were granted an occupational license. Recently, in

Florida, the process has changed and to prevent the confusion of numerous businesses using the same name, the name registry is handled by the state. The zoning review is still a local function.

### Sales and income tax

Selling books is the same as selling any product. Unless you are lucky enough to live in one of the few states that still resists implementing a sales tax, you need to know the rules of, and your responsibilities to, your state Department of Revenue.

In most states whenever anything (except an exempt item) is sold by a business, sales tax is due. There are certain exceptions such as when the buyer is another business that plans to resell the product and has a resale certificate (tax number), or when the purchaser is a tax-exempt organization or entity such as a school or church, or for certain "casual" sales. Because state tax laws are complex, and vary from state to state, talk to your local office for pertinent details.

Keep accurate records of your inventory—where those books removed from inventory went and for what price they sold. Use two- or three- part carbonless sales books and keep the second part for your records. If you are audited by the Department of Revenue you will need this material.

The records of your sales and any personal use of your books will help justify the amount of tax you submit. The amount of tax on each sale is based on the price the buyer pays at the time of purchase, not the list price, and not the unit cost, so be sure you note discounts on your sales slips.

If you apply for a sales tax number, let the tax people know when you plan to open your business so that you don't have to fill out tax reports indicating zero sales for several months prior to receiving your book.

In some states, sales tax is not due when you fill an order from out of state and ship the product to an out-of-state address. Check the rules with your state Department of Revenue or a tax consultant.

### Keeping records

If you are like many creative types, you might imagine that an ideal world is where there are no checkbooks, bank statements, taxes, or the necessity to keep records or receipts. Your time, you think, is more productively spent writing or painting or thinking. The cold cruel world of business should not apply to writers, authors, and publishers. Details …details … details.

Not true—the more organized you can become before your book is produced, the better. If the process seems overwhelming, find someone to help you—a spouse or a friend, or hire a competent bookkeeper. Taking care of the business details is not as difficult as it may seem, and, thanks to user-friendly computer programs such as QuickBooks® or Quicken® you can keep your records up-to-date easily. If you don't use a computer for bookkeeping, get a *Dome Book*® from your local business or office supply store. And, keep your books up to date.

Not only will this help you at income-tax time, but you will be able to track the number of copies you have sold and at what price. In addition to keeping tabs on production expenses, you can track your advertising and marketing costs, and office expenses including postage, stationery, business cards, or brochures. And at the end of each reporting period you will see how much profit or loss you have from your original investment. Keep in mind that you will be able to deduct the expenses of your publishing venture from your gross sales on Schedule C of your IRS 1040 form, but you will need accurate and complete records to prove your claims.

And, finally, the IRS expects you to make a profit on your business at least one year out of three, or you will not be able to claim your business losses against your other income.

**The carton mountain**

Long before you pace the floor waiting for your delivery, you must decide where you are going to store your books. If the bulk of the shipment is going to a distributor, and the rest to you, make sure your packager has the shipping addresses and instructions.

If you are taking only a few cartons for your own use, storage is probably not a problem. However, if you are planning to receive a large number of boxes, you will probably want to make arrangements for an air-conditioned storage unit. If you are lucky enough to live in an area with low humidity and are planning to store the books in the garage, keep them off the floor, dry, and away from things that might spill on, or run into them.

### Shrink-wrap

While we're talking about storing your books in a clean, dry place, we suggest you have at least some of your press run shrink-wrapped.

 Keep a clipboard and pencil handy with your cartons so that you can keep a running tally of the number of boxes you have in stock. Don't open more than one box at a time and make a note of each time you take books out of inventory. That will make it much easier for you to count your inventory at year-end.

 Make sure your packager arranges to have your books packed in quantities you can comfortably lift or handle.

Shrink-wrap is a clear, waterproof, plastic wrap placed around your books before they leave the manufacturer. It shrinks to fit tightly when heated gently, and is airtight and moisture-proof. The advantages of shrink-wrap go beyond storage protection—it may enhance the book's salability. Some buyers like to get books packaged individually, especially coffee-table books. Bookstores will often buy a full package rather than have you break it open for a copy or two. Talk with your packager about the cost of shrink-wrapping per book or per package of five or six books.

The disadvantage, aside from the extra cost, is that you will have to break the wrap to get individual copies of your book. To solve that problem, have a few cartons packed with loose copies.

### Mailing materials and shipping

If you are doing your own mailings, make sure the books are well wrapped so they do not rub against each other, or on the envelope or carton—an advantage of shrink-wrapping. Use padded envelopes to protect your books from becoming scratched or damaged in transit. We purchase several sizes of sturdy boxes from a carton manufacturer so that we can quickly pack several common order sizes without having to search for a right-size box or try to jury-rig or pad out an odd-sized empty box from the liquor or grocery store.

We had shipping labels printed with our company name and address to save time in preparing shipments and to give our product a professional image. Sadly, even sturdy cartons won't protect your

While *TeleVisionaries,* detailing the history of public television, was being printed, self-publisher Jim Robertson did a direct-mail campaign to public television stations, libraries, and the individuals he had targeted as prospective buyers of his book. The anticipated delivery date was mid-December. To capture holiday sales, Robertson wanted to promise delivery in time for Christmas. He did his homework. He took the measurements and weight of his large, hardbound tome to a pack-and-ship store and purchased several hundred mailing cartons. He addressed labels as orders came in and fastened them to the boxes. When the finished books were delivered (on time, thanks to a special effort by the book manufacturer), Robertson signed and numbered the copies in his limited first edition, and he and his wife, Anabel, (who had done all her holiday shopping extra early) prepared the books for mailing and took them to the shipping store. Because all the details had been arranged in advance, *TeleVisionaries* was sent out on schedule and the customers received their Christmas presents on time.

product from uncaring postal clerks. And, when books are damaged in shipping—being bent, dented or getting scratched covers—they will be returned to you, at your expense, by the bookstore, wholesaler or distributor.

Get peel-and-stick labels printed that read, "Complimentary copy, not for resale," or "Review copy." Put them in a obvious spot on the front cover of your damaged returns, then use them for promotional or review purposes. Obviously you do not want stacks of damaged books, so careful packing for shipping is important, as is the selection of a shipping company.

One economical way to get books and other material delivered quickly is the U.S. Postal Service's priority mail. The free, but flimsy, cardboard envelope can be stuffed with anything you can fit into it and sent for the "two-day fee" (at this printing, three dollars). You will do best if you reinforce the bottom and the top with a strip of three-inch packing tape.

United Parcel Service and Airborne Express have instituted an overnight, all-you-can-pack-into-a-special envelope. Airborne's can be obtained prepaid so you just put them in a drop box. Check with other delivery services for their comparable prices.

If you are not using a distributor or a fulfillment house, consider making arrangements with a neighborhood pack-and-ship store to handle your book shipments.

 Save and recycle packing materials for your own shipping. This includes sturdy cartons, "popcorn," envelopes, cardboard, and plastic bubble pads. Some people buy a paper shredder for the office, then save the shredded paper to use for packing.

 If you are sending material to another country, make sure you are using an international express service. The postal service can express your package only to the U.S. border. It cannot guarantee express mail delivery beyond that point.

Special fourth class (book rate) or bound printed matter (a ten pound limit) is much cheaper, but material sent this way travels by ground transportation only. If you are in a hurry, use first class priority. It goes by air. A note on recent developments here. Since the increase in terrorist bombings, the Federal Aviation Administration (FAA) and the U.S. Postal Service have announced that all packages that weigh more than sixteen ounces, being shipped by air in an aircraft carrying passengers (Priority and First-class mail), must be passed *over the counter* at the Post Office or handed to your carrier. Don't drop them in a drop box, they will come right back. Rules are similar, but not as stringent, for the courier services like FedEx, UPS, Airborne Express, etc. as their consignments travel in aircraft that do not carry passengers.

David Dunn, president of Dunn & Company, Inc., in Clinton, Massachusetts, is one of the most resourceful people who has addressed Florida Publishers Association seminars. He has a book "repair" business that can replace covers and pages after the press run has been delivered and a problem has been discovered. Dunn is also eloquent on how to save money shipping your books. You can contact him for a rate chart (See Appendix B.), or do some leg work yourself to see how you can save by shipping your book orders by various designations or combinations of classifications, or by United Parcel Service and some of the other alternative delivery services.

# 7 Riding the distribution rollercoaster

*Independent publishers are often so thrilled at the prospect of being picked up by a national distributor that they jump into a relationship without realizing that the publisher may be financing the distributor's operation.* — Christopher Carroll, vice-president of the Florida Publishers Association[14]

OK, YOU HAVE DONE your market research homework before getting your book packaged and you are sure you know who your readers will be. The book is in the final stages of preparation and you expect it to be sent soon for printing and binding. It is time to set up your deals with the bookstores so all those eager readers will be able to rush down and plunk their money on the counter. Down you go to the local mall with galleys in hand, but at one store after another it is the same story: "Where can we buy it?" "Why, you can buy it from me. How many copies can I reserve for you?" "I'm sorry, but we can't buy from you. Which company is doing your distribution?"

In order to get your books into most stores, you will have to have it carried by a distributor or a wholesaler. This chapter will explain the basics of the distribution system and how it will affect the price of your book, your potential profit and the amount of promotional work you will need to do.

## Distributors

Distributors carry your book on a consignment basis. They usually employ a sales force to call on buyers for the chain bookstores and the larger independents. Distributors also supply the wholesalers with your book. There are national distributors, regional distributors and even local distributors. Each services a specific area or market. Some specialize in sales to retail outlets, others service public and private libraries and some sell to educational institutions.

Selling your book through a distributor will probably return the lowest net profit per copy but it might be the avenue to more sales than any other selling method. A good distribution sales network covers more territory than you can and in a more personal way than the wholesalers can.

Typically an author/publisher will receive about 35 percent of the retail price of each book sold. The other 65 percent is divided between the discount to the bookstore (usually 40 percent), the salesperson's commission (5–10 percent), shipping and overhead, and the distributor's profit. This means if you are planning to sell even *some* of your books through a distributor, you need to set the price at least three- to- four- times the production cost just to break even; more if you want to cover marketing costs and make a profit.

Unless distributor sales are going to be your major sales method, breaking even on these sales is probably OK. You will make full profit on those books that you sell on your own at cover price, and some profit on those you sell discounted to organizations or markets not covered by your agreement.

Distributors usually expect an exclusive arrangement with you; in other words you can't sign on with more than one distributor unless they are noncompetitive. For example, if your distributor does not sell to the library market, you may be able to sign on with a library distributor also. Usually

The distributor you choose can give you important counsel prior to the completion of your book. Work with your book packager and distributor on concepts for your title and cover. The salespeople in the field are an invaluable resource. Consider any tips they give you to make your product more marketable.

You typically will not be limited in your opportunities to sell to stores other than bookstores. Gift shops, card stores, tourist traps and specialty stores are a lucrative market and you should work them hard. Figure on promoting your product at every appropriate store within a half-day drive of your home. Make follow-up visits every three months or when you are called.

you are not allowed to sell on your own to any bookstores except maybe to your local independent. The reasoning behind this is: If the distributor's salespeople are to be enticed to work hard to sell your book, they must have the exclusive right to sell. Nothing deflates a salesperson faster than to give his pitch to a buyer, only to find out that the customer has already bought your title from someone else. The distributor's salespeople should be calling on the major independents, the buyers for the chains and the wholesalers.

Even if you think you have a sizzling topic and the hottest book of the season, the distributor will want to know what your marketing budget and publicity plans are that will help generate sales. That's right, *your* plans! And *your* budget. Don't be surprised if larger distributors expect you to be ready to spend a lot of money to promote your book. The salespeople want to know your marketing plans because their customers, the book buyers, will ask. Your plans, backed by your advertising and marketing dollars, will have a major effect on the sales of the book in their stores. Books that receive national attention often have promotional budgets of several hundred thousand dollars. Publishers count on that kind of money creating the demand for the book. Don't expect the distributor to work in a vacuum.

 Send copies of any reviews or articles about you or your book to your distributor. They will make copies to send to the salespeople in the field. Anything to give an extra boost to sales is appreciated.

Distributors usually print catalogs of their titles, with annotations and ordering information, twice each year, in January and July. These catalogs are timed to reach the buyers in plenty of time to order for the Christmas holidays and for the summer reading period. Publishers in the distribution network are often asked to participate by buying a page (or more) to highlight their offerings. These pages vary in cost depending on their placement in the catalog and the number of colors in the print job. Sometimes partial pages are available.

Even though you would like to see your book featured in a catalog, be realistic about its sales potential and do not commit for an ad that will cost more than the profit you will receive from the books sold. If you do not want a display ad, your title will simply be listed in the catalog of titles by subject area. Unfortunately, the sales people do not spend much time trying to sell from the list.

One major advantage to establishing a relationship with a distributor is that often they also serve as a fulfillment center. A fulfillment center accepts orders by mail or through an 800 line twenty-four hours a day, has credit-card capability, and ships your book directly to the customer. This means that if you are on a radio talk show in Chicago, you can direct listeners to call the 800 number of your distributor or fulfillment center for immediate service. You can also include the 800 number on all your advertisements, on your magnetic signs, and on your business cards. You capture the impulse buyers because they can make that call immediately, and they can charge the book on their credit card. Publishers will generally realize somewhat more profit with fulfillment sales than they will from sales by the sales force because there is no commission. If your distributor does not fulfill, find a fulfillment house to handle your books.

It is important to coordinate your publicity and marketing efforts with the distributor's shipping schedule so that you are not creating a demand for the book in an area before it is actually available. For instance, if you are planning to be a guest on a talk show in St. Louis, let the distributor know beforehand so he can alert his sales force in the listening area. They will then be able to

"Keep in mind that distribution agreements are negotiable, so don't necessarily jump at the first offer you receive. Make certain you know *all* the costs of doing business with a distributor," is sound advice from Christopher Carroll, vice-president of the Florida Publishers Association, and sales manager for Publishers Media Services.

There is no "best" way to sell a book. Analyze your topic and your marketing plans to realistically determine if you need a distributor, wholesaler or fulfillment house. Talk with other independent or self-publishers about what has worked well for them. If you decide to sign up with a distributor or wholesaler, check all contract terms, and ask about insurance and returns.

make sure local bookstores have your book to display and sell before, during and after the show. If you can follow up with personal appearances you will increase your sales.

Distributors usually pay publishers three months after the month the books were sold. Some try to stretch the term longer than that. Do not count on a fast cash flow.

## Wholesalers

Why do most bookstores purchase only from wholesalers rather than directly from authors or publishers or even distributors? Because it is good business. Wholesalers will stock, or at least make available virtually every title in *Books In Print*. Any number of titles from various publishers can be put on a single invoice and into one shipment, saving time and money for both the shipper and the receiver.

If you want to make your book widely available to bookstores, you *must* have your title available through a wholesaler such as Ingram Book Company or Baker & Taylor (See the appendixes for a more complete list). Some bookstores only order from wholesalers, so your distributor should try to place your book title with them first. Many wholesalers have a selection process. Ingram has a selection committee that reviews new titles. The process may be waived if the publisher has a large guaranteed order for the book. This book was accepted by Ingram at the same time that Barnes & Noble recommended that *Smart Self-Publishing* be stocked nationwide in all the Barnes & Noble superstores and most of the B. Dalton Booksellers mall stores.

Typically wholesalers will ask small publishers for a 55 percent discount, and also will expect them to pay the costs of shipping the books to the wholesale warehouse. The good news is that these usually are not consignment sales. Wholesalers usually *buy* your books to carry in their stock (that is why they have the selection process). The bad news is that you have to wait ninety days for your money, will be required to accept returns (wholesalers also must accept returns from bookstores for damage, overstock or poor sales) and either issue credit to the wholesaler or take a charge against money due you. Expect receiving inspectors to be picky about damage and what they will accept.

If your promotion schedule falters or demand dwindles, large numbers of returns can come in *after* you have received (and spent) your money. You will then end up with a debit on your account and will have to return money to the wholesaler or distributor. It can happen to the Big Guys just as well as to unknowns or small presses.

Newt Gingrich's science fiction book, *1945*, is one recent release that did not meet publisher expectations. For every one hundred copies that were distributed, eighty-one were returned, according to an Associated Press story quoting publisher Jim Baen. At the time the story was written, Baen had 97,000 copies of *1945* still in storage[15].

Even though book wholesalers do not have a sales force out knocking on doors, they may also produce a catalog of their titles. As with distributor catalogs, publishers are invited to buy space. Wholesalers also rely on publisher's hype to create the demand for the book and generate orders.

Small publishers have learned the hard way that the regional offices and warehouses of some national wholesalers operate virtually independently of each other. They do not share inventory information, and do not fill orders received by other warehouses for books that are out of stock at the other warehouse, even though they may be overstocked and about to return the same title to the publisher. If you can, be sure that your book is available at each of the wholesaler's distribution centers, or at least in every one that services an area in which you are going to publicize your book.

If you do not have a distributor yet, or cannot get one to carry your book, try contacting the wholesale companies directly (Addresses are in Appendix B.) to find out how you can get your title listed. If you do not anticipate wide readership, ask if the wholesaler has a system for ordering only on request and paying you cash with the order. Ingram has the "Green Light" program set up to stock one or two copies of a book so the company can quickly fill an order, then, when a copy is sold, the title can quickly be reordered from the publisher. Some publishers offer to give wholesalers a larger discount price in exchange for accepting no returns.

Like any other aspect of producing or selling your book, you will want to ask for references before you commit yourself to an exclusive arrangement with any distributor or wholesaler and, even then, insist on the right to cancel with reasonable notice. Call some of the publishers the firm represents and see if they are satisfied with the service.

Some distributors and wholesalers pay according to their contract schedule. Others are notoriously difficult to deal with, leaving small publishers with no payments, a lot of extra charges, confusing accounting systems and concern that publishers have lost control of their inventory and their investment. Make sure you know all the potential costs, including your marketing effort, from the outset.

## Reaching the library market

There are a number of distributors that specialize in library sales. Two of the best are Unique Books and Quality Books, both very helpful, and eager to include mainstream books from small publishers in their lines.

Library distributors are full of good information that can help you make your book more salable. Like other distributors, their salespeople carry a portfolio of covers and annotations, rather than boxes of sample books.

Librarians and library distributors have told us that, contrary to popular belief, libraries *are* purchasing softcover books. Softcover editions are less costly so libraries on limited budgets are able to buy more books. Many books, especially best-sellers and others that may become dated, circulate only a set number of times before they are removed or replaced.

Librarian Helen Burns tells us patrons will often look at a book in the library to "try before they buy." She shares these tips on marketing to libraries and their customers:

✓ Include the ISBN and price on your literature. Don't abbreviate or hide them. The easier you make it to buy your book the more apt I am to buy it

✓ Include an order form or coupon, but be sure to say *not* to tear it out, but to make a copy. Every week satisfied readers ask me how they can buy a title for themselves.

✓ If possible, include an 800 number as a service to customers who wish to buy the item.

However, library reviewers will not include your personal phone number. That is viewed as advertising.

- ✓ Don't promote the book to me and then tell me it is out-of-stock, then send me another flier and another out-of-stock notice.

- ✓ Consider your audience. Teenagers love paperbacks, while senior citizens who have arthritic hands thoughtfully evaluate the weight and size of a book.

- ✓ Spend time on your title. Test it on family and friends. Do they remember the correct title? Be sure that the title reflects the content of the book.

- ✓ If it is a nonfiction book, always have an index.

- ✓ If fiction, relate it to another well-known title.

- ✓ Name recognition of your company is important and can help sell your books.

- ✓ Provide personal information on the author. This makes the books easier to sell to the library public.

- ✓ Go where librarians gather and promote to them directly. For example, at a conference arrange for a readers theater featuring your book. Set up chairs and arrange for refreshments. Share the book and/or presentations with fellow authors.

- ✓ Provide bookmarks promoting your title. Librarians always look for new, and inexpensive marketing methods.

The more information librarians have about your books, the more likely they are to recommend them to their patrons. Librarians will hear about your book from the publicity you generate and from the public's reaction to it. Titles are often purchased as a result of an interview in a newspaper or magazine, a radio talk show or even a speech to a local club.

Finally, our librarian friends tell us that it's OK to market directly to them. They will purchase books they know their patrons will like right from you, especially if your book isn't available from a distributor's salesperson. It helps if you learn the demographics of the particular library. Librarians work cooperatively with each other and will tell their colleagues about books that are doing well.

The staff at Quality Books emphasizes that while North America's libraries "annually spend billions of dollars for books and videos," it is very hard to reach the individual librarians. Because librarians are faced with selecting from among 60,000 new titles published annually, a full-service library distribution service, working by appointment, can help sell your book.

### The vanishing independent bookstore

More and more smaller independent bookstores, including some of the wonderful ones that have been in business for decades, are being forced to close their doors, overwhelmed by the competition from book superstores and the major discount outlets. Even the chain bookstores in some major shopping malls are suffering from lost sales due to the heavy discounts offered

> Books-A-Million, a rapidly-growing superstore chain based in the Southeast, allows their managers the flexibility to buy directly from authors and small publishers, but most chains, such Barnes & Noble or Waldenbooks, Borders, and even many independents require titles to be carried by a distributor or wholesaler.
>
> It is tough to get your book accepted by the chains. Many buyers will not return phone calls or acknowledge the receipt of your materials. Be persistent if you think your book belongs in the chains. You will also need to have a distributor or wholesaler for chains to buy from, and for your book to be carried by a distributor, it *must* have an ISBN and bar code.

at the Sam's Clubs, Kmarts and superstores nearby. Readers who are looking for bargains rather than a wide selection of titles are attracted to the discount stores by deeply discounted best-sellers. The impact of the discounts particularly affects independent publishers and self-publishers who, because of high unit cost, cannot easily compete with the aggressive discount structure. It is important to learn how your book fits into both the independents and the superstores.

Many independents are able to buy books directly from an author, but they want to purchase only a quality product, and they want to buy under the same terms that they do with the wholesalers. If you can sell directly to a bookstore, expect to give them a discount of

40 percent from the cover price. Often they will pay at the time of purchase. The larger independents usually buy the same as the chain stores do—only from wholesalers.

## Consignment sales to other retail outlets

Often when you approach the owner or manager of a store—it can be a small bookstore or any other type—they will want to place your book on consignment. You should know that consignment sales can be risky. Many things can happen, not the least of which is that you forget where the books are and never go back to collect.

If you do leave your books be sure you get a signed receipt from someone who has the authority to give it and that you have it in writing that the store will be responsible for the retail price minus the agreed upon discount (usually no more than 25 percent) for each book that is not returned in salable condition. Try to service your consignment accounts once each month at a time you know the owner or manager will be there to pay you and/or order more books.

## Commission reps

Wanda Jewell, executive director of the Southeast Booksellers Association is emphatic about consignments. "Don't ever put a book on consignment," she said. Instead she suggests working with a commission representative to hype and sell your book.

Publishers Marketing Association says working with a commission rep can be expensive, but is "by far the most effective means of getting books into the book trade....The best reps are very sophisticated players in the book industry....About 60 percent of them belong to a professional organization called the National Association of Independent Publishers Representatives." PMA suggests that you may want to get the NAIPR pamphlet called "Sell-

 Linda was in the midst of a booksigning at a local B. Dalton Booksellers when a man stopped, picked up her books, looked through them, and handed her his business card. He said, "Call my buyer and tell her I said to order your books." It turned out that he ran a distribution service in the Midwest that supplies books to newsstands and bookstores. The service bought two sixty-book cartons of each book—outright. If only all sales were that easy!

ing on Commission: Guidelines for Publishers" and the organization's membership directory. SEBA's membership directory also includes the names of a number of commission reps. Wanda Jewell suggests contacting the individuals listed for their "rules." (See Appendix B for a list of commission reps.)

## Newsstand services

There are many small, regional distributors or jobbers who service newsstands, airports, chain gift shops or grocery stores. If a location, such as an airport or hotel gift shop, seems like a good one for your title, then find out what company supplies these books and try to get your book accepted for their line. Some of these distributors are easier to "crack" than others.

## Specialty outlets

Certain books lend themselves best to sales in specialty stores or catalogs—such as cookbooks, books on women's issues, ethnic books, environmental subjects, and gay and lesbian issues. The National Park Service has gift shops that sell topical history and regional books. Books about animals will find a market at zoos or aquariums.

And, there is a tremendous market for religious and New Age spiritual books in Christian bookstores, and specialty shops.

There are also many niche distributors such as New Leaf, which specializes in new age and related spiritual topics. Find out the names of regional distributors from bookstores, libraries, other publishers, or publishing associa-

An author we know self-published a nicely packaged, well-illustrated children's book that had a Christian—or at least deity—message in it. A friend took copies of the book to a local Christian bookstore. The clerk's first question was: "What scripture does it relate to?" The friend tried to explain that the message was one of accepting all people for what they are. But the clerk said the store was not interested unless a specific reference was printed on the cover. If conspicuously printing a scripture reference helps sell the book, then do it!

tions. You may find that your book will fit in. For example, Mickler's Floridiana is a wholesale distributor of books on Florida topics and has an extensive catalog.

*Big Books from Small Presses,* a catalog published by Upper Access Books, Hinesburg, Vermont, lists 350 or so selected nonfiction titles—all published by author/ publishers and small independent presses.

Lisa and Steve Carlson, owners of Upper Access, started publishing with one book in 1987. Even though their book received nationwide publicity on "Donahue" and in the *New York Times,* they found it difficult to get the book into bookstores because they were unable to sustain the momentum. Knowing other small publishers were faced with the same difficulty, they started the *Big Books from Small Presses* catalog, which now has more than 30,000 subscribers and is well-received by book buyers around the country.

Upper Access offers fulfillment services, taking credit card orders twenty-four-hours-a-day by 800 number, and they sell a software program, Publishers Invoice and Information Generating System (PIIGS), for small publishers.

Upper Access was featured in *Publisher's Report,* a publication of the National Association of Independent Publishers, as a company that has helped hundreds of independent publishers and self-publishers. Send a review copy or promotional material to them to see if your book will fit their line.

We'll say it again. Writing the book may be the easiest part of the project. If a book is not properly produced, it will not make it into the distribution system which serves the bookstore market. Self-publishers must understand the book marketplace in order to break even or make a small profit when books are sold at a 65 percent discount from the retail price through a distributor.

We've known a number of authors who have literally walked away from their "baby" expecting it to sell simply because it was in a distributor's catalog or carried by a wholesaler. They are usually disappointed, and blame everyone else for the book's failure. Authors must help make sales happen, either through their own efforts, or by paying someone else to do it.

# 8 Summing things up

*By studying authoritative books on self-publishing, attending publishers' seminars, networking with other self-publishers, and learning about the nontraditional markets for books, the smart self-publisher increases the odds of success.* — Betsy Lampé, National Association of Independent Publishers.

THERE IS MUCH MORE to creating a book than writing it! Being a smart self-publisher is a combination of being a good consumer, putting your trust in the right people, and understanding the realities of the world of books.

One way to tap into valuable resources is to become a part of a network of self-publishers and small independent presses. Members of these groups have had the same problems you are facing. They are happy to answer your questions and share ideas on such issues as marketing and distribution. You may be able to join cooperatively sponsored tables at trade shows or attend informative seminars. Those publishers with books in progress will be able to take advantage of tips and pointers before their book goes to press. Those whose books are already off press can network about marketing.

Many regions in the country have organizations for publishers—some are listed in the appendix. We are members of the National Association of Independent Publishers (NAIP), founded by Betty Wright, the Southeast Booksellers Association (SEBA), the Florida Publishers Association (FPA) and Publishers Marketing Association (PMA). If your state does not have a publishers association, join NAIP and start your own group, or join any of the associations listed in the appendix.

The NAIP sponsors an annual new book contest, and offers a bimonthly, information-packed newsletter in which new books are announced. The newsletter also provides marketing and publicity leads, contacts for talk shows and names of reviewers.

The FPA sponsors at least two well-attended seminars, called Edu-Conferences, each year. Experts on indexing, book repairs, foreign rights, publicity and marketing, cover design and distribution have been among the speakers. The organization also publishes a bimonthly newsletter that is sent to members and produces a catalog/directory that is distributed at trade shows, and mailed to libraries and bookstores.

Members of the networking organizations are more diverse than just author/publishers. They also represent vendors—distributors, marketers, agents, book manufacturers, cover designers and

*The Florida Publishers Association cooperative display at the 1994 ABA tradeshow.*

typesetters—who have time to answer individual questions.

What better way to learn about the "real world" of selling books than from Fred Ciporen, publisher of *Publishers Weekly* or from

regional buyers for bookstores. Seminar round-table discussions offer question and answer sessions on a wide variety of topics, and often attendees find new outlets for selling their books. That is something we all want to do! The appendix lists many regional associations that you may join.

We also urge you to join organizations sponsored by associated groups, such as the Southeast Booksellers Association (SEBA). Their newsletters are a valuable source of information on many business trends and topics and, if you attend their trade shows, especially as an exhibitor, you will have the opportunity to meet the people who buy books.

## Trade shows

At the shows you will receive good exposure for your book. And, another benefit—you will make direct contact with many bookstore owners and buyers, and learn firsthand what types of books they are looking for and how they order their stock. Be sure to get their business cards, then follow up shortly after the show with a direct mailing reiterating your special show discount terms or perhaps offering special payment terms like a 90 day billing for holiday orders.

Many publishers have a drawing for a book or other gift to encourage show attendees to leave a card at the booth. As a part of your booth, have your books, promotional literature and a special trade-show discount posted. You may want to have bookmarks printed that display your book's cover and ordering information. And be ready to write orders.

It is also very important to ask attendees questions about their

*The Tabby House exhibit and display at the 1996 SEBA trade show at the Opryland Hotel in Nashville, Tennessee*

stores and chains to find out if your book will fit their line.

If you have done your marketing homework and have produced a professional product, you should be able to find a number of appropriate outlets for your book.

You can also purchase mailing lists generated by the trade show organizations and do your own direct mail, targeted at bookstores. The independent book store association in Colorado has a free brochure that lists members and their addresses.

Some of the large trade shows, such as that of the former American Booksellers Association (ABA), which was recently sold and renamed BookExpo America, are costly for small presses. Consider sharing a booth with other publishers and authors to offset the expense and to give you time to roam the floor.

PMA offers cooperative display and advertising opportunities for members. It also produces an informative monthly newsletter for independent publishers. Executive Director Jan Nathan is refreshingly candid in reporting on the outcome of PMA's participation in various trade shows, such as ABA.

PMA also offers a trade distribution program for new titles to help small presses get new titles (that have not already been presented and rejected) into the chains.

And, finally, when working the shows, wear comfortable shoes, as you will need to be on your feet for ten or twelve hours each day. Few books are ever sold while the booth attendant is sitting down.

### Giving up the myths

This brings us full circle in the premise of this book. Smart self-publishing means making a commitment to producing a professional product, developing a marketing strategy and a being willing to promote your book. For most unknown authors, it means giving up these oft-heard notions:

✓A self-published author is inferior to one who has yet to be discovered.
✓Someone else should invest in and sell my book. Authors should not have to get involved in sales.

Betsy Lampé, executive director of the NAIP says, "Self-publishers are 'born' for a variety of reasons. As the large New York publishing houses reduce the number of authors in their 'stables,' those rejected by them continue to seek publication and often turn to producing their work themselves. Other authors become publishers just to maintain control of their work and its production. Some authors just want to make the lion's share of profits from works they know are marketable. And there are yet others who use self-publishing as a tool to start a publishing house, with an eye toward publishing the works of others.

"In fact, Cahners Direct Marketing approximates that eight thousand individuals per year set out on the self-publishing trail. With careful planning and execution of the projects, many of the eight thousand will be successful."

Times are changing, and even the Big Guys are scouting for successful self-published books to buy for their lines. They are impressed by the entrepreneurial spirit of the self-publishers, especially if they can see proven sales results. You will give your book a better chance to succeed on its own or being picked up by a larger publisher if you do it right. That message is underscored by the following editorial that was written by Christopher Carroll for the June 1995 issue of the Florida Publishers Association newsletter. We are reprinting it with permission.

"As independent publishers, we often feel discriminated against and at a disadvantage when competing with the mega-publishers. Wholesalers and distributors often resist stocking our titles. Bookstores won't buy our books. If they do, they only buy a couple of copies and display them spine out in the wrong section of the store. *Publishers Weekly* won't review our titles. And it's like pulling teeth to get an editor to write a feature story about one of our authors. In short, life is pretty rough for independent publishers.

"We could respond to these inequities by giving up. Or by taking the offensive and fighting for what we feel is our due."

Carroll continued, "I would contend that a third option, in the end, will do more to advance our cause. That option is to work within the system that is already in place, instead of expecting the system to flex to meet our needs.

"If we want wholesalers and distributors to stock our titles, it is our responsibility to develop books which have obvious value, that includes properly designed covers with the author and title displayed on the spine, and bar codes on the back. We must get the word out to bookstores to create a demand for our books. If we want to sell to bookstores, we need to make the public want to buy our books through promotion. If we want our books reviewed, we need to get review copies or bound galleys to the magazines at least three months in advance of the publication date. And, if we want feature articles written about our books and authors, we need to get the word out to the editors.

"In short, if we want the same treatment that the big publishers get, we need to act like professional publishers. Instead of bucking the system, we would do more good for our companies, and for the image of all independent publishers, if we learn to fit into the professional publishing community."

## You can be a smart self-publisher

The publishing business can be a grand adventure fulfilling a life dream, or it can be fraught with discouragement and cartons of books stored in the garage. We've tried to provide some basic knowledge of what the marketplace is like, and what you can do to find satisfaction in your project.

Do your marketing homework. Produce a professional product acceptable to retail and distribution outlets.

Be realistic about your press run and the price. If you do not feel confident enough to do it on your own, find and hire a competent book packaging company, at least for your first book—but don't forget to check their references.

Commit yourself to being actively involved in the sale of the book. If you don't do it, who will? Finally, network with others in the publishing field. It doesn't matter if they are one-book publishers or real professionals. Pick their brains for ideas, and let them pick yours. A great thing about publishing—most publishers aren't trying to sell the same product, and therefore are not in competition with each other. They like to help each other!

And remember, there is self-publishing and there is *smart* self-publishing. You can be one of the smart ones!

# Endnotes

1. Printed in the August 16, 1991 issue of the *Sarasota Herald-Tribune*

2. *Publishers Weekly*, Februrary 14, 1994

3. The *New York Times*, December 26, 1994

4. *Publishers Weekly*, April 29, 1996

5. *Publishers Weekly*, May 25, 1995

6. *U.S. News & World Report*, June 8, 1992

7. National Public Radio, "All Things Considered," December 20, 1994

8. *While Morningstars Sang*, and *A Place of Springs*, cooperative anthologies published by Tabby House

9. Strathmoor Books, 1997

10. Lucia Staniels, publicist

11. Florida Publishers Association Newsletter, June 1995

12. *Aldus* magazine, July/August issue, 1995

13. Florida Publishers Association meeting, March 1994

14. FPA Newsletter, June 1995

15. Associated Press story in the *Sarasota Herald-Tribune*, August 3, 1996

# Appendix A

## Must-have references

- *The Chicago Manual of Style, The Essential Guide for Writers, Editors and Publishers.* 14th ed., Edited by John Grossman. Chicago: University of Chicago Press, 1993.

- *The Associated Press Stylebook and Libel Manual.* New York: The Associated Press.

- Webster's Tenth New Collegiate *Dictionary.* Springfield, Mass.: G & C. Merriam.

- *Literary Market Place/The Directory of the American Book Publishing Industry.* New York: R.R. Bowker. Annual comprehensive listing of book publishers, agents and other resources.

## A short list of handy sources

- Bates, Jefferson. *Writing with Precision.* Washington D.C.: Acropolis Books, 1993.

- Bernstein, Theodore M. *The Careful Writer, a Modern Guide to English Usage.* New York: Atheneum, 1965.

- Bodian, Nat. *The Joy of Publishing.* Fairfield, Iowa: Open Horizons, 1996.

- Borden, Kay. *Bulletproof News Releases.* Marietta, Ga.: Franklin-Serrate Publishers, 1994.

- Castro, Elizabeth. *HTML for the World Wide Web.* Berkeley, Calif.: Peachpit Press, 1996. Great for setting up Web pages. Easy for the beginner to read and understand.

- Crawford, Tad. *Business and Legal Forms for Authors and Self-Publishers.* Allworth, 1990.

- *All-in-One Directory.* New Paltz, N.Y.: Gebbie Press. Lists media sources; available on disk.

- Hacker, Diana. *A Writer's Reference.* Boston: St. Martin's Press, 1989.

- Kirsch, Jonathan. *Handbook of Publishing Law.* Acrobat Books, 1995.

- Kremer, John. *1001 Ways to Market your Books.* Fairfield, Iowa: Ad-Lib Publications, 1993.

- Neiderst, Jennifer, with Edie Freedman.
  *Designing for the Web: Getting Started in a New Medium.*
  Sebastol, Calif,:
  O'Reilly and Associates, 1996.

- Parker, Steve.
  *Web Page Creator*
  www.webus.com/wpc
  Build you own Web page with this user-friendly software. Download from World Wide Web.

- Plotnik, Arthur.
  *The Elements of Editing; A Modern Guide for Editors and Journalists.*
  New York: Collier Books, 1982.

- Poynter, Dan and Mindy Bingham.
  *Is there a book inside you? A step-by-step plan for writing your book.*
  4th ed.
  Santa Barbara, Calif.:
  Para Publishing, 1996.

- Poynter, Dan.
  *The Self-Publishing Manual: How to Write, Print and Sell Your Own Books.* 9th ed.
  Santa Barbara, Calif.:
  Para Publishing, 1996.

- Ross, Marilyn and Tom.
  *Jump Start Your Book's Sales: Revolutionary, Relentless, Result-getting Marketing and Publicity Strategies for Authors and Publishers.*
  Buena Vista, Colo.:
  Communication Creativity.

- Ross, Marilyn and Tom.
  *The Complete Guide to Self-Publishing,* 3rd. ed.
  Buena Vista, Colo.:
  Communication Creativity, 1994.

- Smith, Ronald Ted.
  *Book Publishing Encyclopedia.*
  Sarasota, Fla.:
  BookWorld Press, 1996.

- Strunk, William and E.B. White.
  *The Elements of Style.* 3rd ed.
  New York: Macmillan Publishing Co., 1979.

**Subscription suggestions**

- *Book Marketing Update*
  209 S. Main Street
  P.O. Box 205
  Fairfield, IA 52556-0205
  (515) 472-6130
  (800) 796-6130
  fax (515) 472-1560
  JohnKremer@aol.com
  www.bookmarket.com
  Published by John Kremer. Latest marketing information and tips, review and distribution sources, books on publishing.

- Jeffrey Lant Associates
  P.O. Box 38-2767
  Cambridge, MA 02238
  (617) 546-6372
  fax-on-demand: (403) 425-6049
  webmaster@worldprofit.com.
  Free newsletter. Marketing books.

- *Publishing Poynters* newsletter
  Para Publishing,
  Dan Poynter, publisher
  P.O. Box 8206
  Santa Barbara, CA 93118-8206
  (805) 968-7277
  fax-on-demand: (805) 968-8947
  Orders: (800) PARAPUB
  fax (general): (805) 968-1379
  DanPoynter@ParaPublishing.com
  www.ParaPublishing.com
  An outstanding source of
  marketing news and tips. Also has a
  fax-on-demand service, books,
  workshops, mailing lists, and many
  free documents. Watch for his
  seminars and visit his Web site.

- *Small Publisher*
  c/o Nigel Maxey
  Box 1620
  Pineville, WV 24874
  (304) 732-8195
  Bimonthly. Chock-full of marketing
  ideas, and helpful tips. Good
  information, good price

- *Publishers Weekly*
  P.O. Box 6457
  Torrence, CA 90504
  (800) 278-2991
  fax (310) 978-6901
  Know the trends in the publishing
  industry, includes occasional
  commentary about self-publishing.
  Subscription is increasingly
  expensive, but the info is good.

- *Small Press Magazine* and
  *Publishing Entrepreneur*
  121 E. Front St. Suite 401
  Traverse City, MI 49684
  (616) 933-0445
  fax (616) 933-0448
  jenkins.group@smallpress.com
  Provides bimonthly publications,
  information, and education services
  to publishers and institutions.

  *Small Press.* Prominent trade review
  publication for the independent
  publishing sector.

  *Publishing Entrepreneur* diagrams
  lucrative entrepreneurial
  opportunities.

- *Publisher's Report,* newsletter of
  the National Association of
  Independent Publishers
  P.O. Box 430
  Highland City, FL 33846-0430
  (941) 648-4420 (phone/fax)
  NAIP@aol.com
  Worth joining NAIP for the
  outstanding newsletter!

- *PMA Newsletter*
  2401 Pacific Coast Hwy. Ste.102
  Hermosa Beach, CA 90254
  (310) 372-2732
  fax (310)374-3342
  PMAOnline@aol.com
  Excellent compendium of
  information from the Publishers
  Marketing Association. Good
  articles.

- *Span Connection*
  P.O. Box 1306-LIST
  Buena Vista, CO 81211-1306
  (719) 395-4790
  fax (719) 395-8374
  span@span-assn.org
  A newsletter published by publishing experts Tom and Marilyn Ross for members of the Small Publishers Association of North America.

## Review sources

We strongly urge that you look for nontraditional review sources to promote your book, rather relying on the ones used by the Big Guys. It is hard to compete. Also, submit your professionally produced book to catalogs that promote your topic. If your topic is a hunting adventure story, seek out magazines and/or catalogs that specialize in outdoor adventure or hunting.

- *Bas Bleu, Inc.* Bookseller by Post
  1447 Peachtree St, Ste. 508
  Atlanta, GA 30309
  (404) 874-0053; (800) 433-1155
  fax (404)874-270
  A delightful, well-written catalog which contains short reviews by readers. Books considered for catalog must be well-produced, hard-to-find, cannot proselytize, usually in category of fiction, travel, humor, children's literature, biography, cooking, gardening.

- *Publishers Weekly* "Forecasts"
  att: Jonathan Bing
  249 W. 17th St.
  New York, NY 10011
  (212) 463-6782
  fax (212) 463-6631
  Submit bound galleys or page proofs at least three months before publication.

- *ALA Booklist*
  50 E. Huron St.
  Chicago, IL 60611
  (312) 944-6780
  fax (312) 337-6787
  Librarians pay attention to ALA reviews.

- *Kirkus Reviews*
  200 Park Ave. S.
  New York, NY 10003
  (212) 777-4554
  Primarily reviews fiction. Send two galleys.

- The *New York Times Book Review*
  229 West 43rd. St.
  New York, NY 10036
  (212) 556-1234

- *USA Today* Book Reviews
  1100 Wilson Boulevard
  Arlington, VA 22209
  (703) 284-6000; (508) 362-3441
  fax (508) 262-5445

# Appendix B

## Useful stuff for self-publishers

These are names of people or companies that we have worked with, plus a number we have learned about at trade shows, some from our publishers association meetings, and some from other publishers. We've tried to make the list up to date at the time we went to press. *Our list is by no means all inclusive nor meant as an endorsement.* We strongly urge that you talk with author/publishers who have used these services within the last two years for references. When deciding on your marketing strategies, weigh the cost of your marketing expenses against your desired outcome.

## Distributors

- American Wholesale Book Co.
  4350 Bryson Blvd.
  Florence, AL 35630
  (205) 766-3789
  fax (205) 764-2511
  Owned by Books-A-Million

- Associated Publishers Group
  1501 County Hospital Road
  Nashville, TN 37218
  (615) 254-2450
  fax (615) 254-2456

- bookazine co., inc
  75 Hook Road
  Bayonne, NJ 07002
  (201) 339-7777
  fax (201) 339-7778

- BookWorld Services, Inc.
  1933 Whitfield Park Loop
  Sarasota, FL 34243
  (941) 758-8094;
  (800) 444-2524;
  fax (941) 753-9396
  www.bookworld.com

- Consortium Book Sales and
  Distribution
  1045 Westgate Drive
  St. Paul, MN 55114-9035
  (612) 221-9035
  fax (612) 221-0124
  cnsrtm@aol.com

- Independent Publishers Group
  814 North Franklin St.
  Chicago, IL 60610
  (312) 337-0747
  fax (312) 337-5985
  ipgbook@mcs.com

- Southern Publishers Group
  P.O. Box 1360
  147 Corporate Way
  Pelham, AL 35124
  (205) 664-6980; (800) 628-0903
  fax (205) 664-6984

- National Book Network, Inc.
  4720 Boston Way
  Lanham, MD 20706
  (301) 731-9525; (800) 462-6420
  fax (301) 459-2118
  www.nbnbooks.com

- New Leaf Distributing Co.
  401 Thornton Road
  Lithia Springs, GA 30057
  (800) 326-2665 for orders
  (770) 948-7845
  fax (800) 326-1066
  www.newleaf-dist.com
  Specializes in new age and spiritual topics.

- Publishers Group West
  4065 Hollis Street
  Emeryville, CA 94608
  (510) 658-3453; (800) 788-3123
  fax (510) 658-1934

- Bookmasters Distribution Services
  1444 U.S. Rt. 42 RD 11
  Mansfield, OH 44903
  (419) 281-1802
  fax (419) 281-6883
  (800) 507-2665 for orders

## Library distributors

- Brodart Co.
  500 Arch Street
  Williamsport, PA 17705
  (717) 326-2461; (800) 233-8467

- The Book House, Inc.
  208 W. Chicago Street
  Jonesville, MI 49250-0125
  (517) 849-2117
  fax (517) 849-9716
  Jobbers serving libraries with any book in print.

- Emery-Pratt Company
  1966 W. Main St.
  Owosso, MI 48867-1372
  (517) 723-5291; (800) 248-3887
  fax (517) 723-4677
  custserv@emery-pratt.com

- Midwest Library Service
  11443 St. Charles Rock Road
  Bridgeton, MO 63044-2789
  (314) 739-3100
  fax (314) 739-1326
  mail@midwestls.com

- Quality Books, Inc.
  1003 W. Pines Road
  Oregon, IL 61061-9680
  (815) 732-4450
  fax (815) 732-4499

- Unique Books
  4230 Grove Ave.
  Gurnee, IL 60031
  (847) 623-9171
  fax (847) 623-7238

- Blackwell North America, Inc.
  100 University Court
  Blackwood, NJ 08012
  (609) 228-8900
  fax (609) 228-6097

## Wholesalers

- Baker & Taylor (warehouse)
  251 Mount Olive Church Road
  Commerce, GA 30599
  (706) 335-5000; (800) 775-1100
  fax (800) 775-7480

- Baker & Taylor (billing department and warehouse)
  501 S. Gladiolus St.
  Momence, IL 60954
  (815) 472-2444; (800) 775-2300
  fax (800) 775-3500
  btinfo@baker-taylor.e-mail.com

- Baker & Taylor (buyers' offices and warehouse)
  50 Kirby Avenue
  Somerville, NJ 08876

- Mickler's Floridiana Inc.
  Sam Mickler, owner
  P.O. Box 62145
  0viedo, FL 32762-1450
  (407) 365-6425; (phone/fax)
  Books about Florida

- Ingram Book Company
  One Ingram Blvd.
  Box 3006
  LaVergne, TN 37086-1986
  (615) 793-5000; (800) 937-8100
  fax (615) 793-3823
  Preferred by Barnes & Noble

- the distributors
  702 S. Michigan St.
  South Bend, IN 46601
  (219) 232-8500
  fax (219) 288-4141
  Actually a wholesaler. Takes books on consignment, pays well and recycles returns when possible.

## Fulfillment

- Upper Access
  Lisa or Steve Carlson
  P.O. Box 457
  Hinesburg, VT 05461
  (802) 482-2988
  fax (802) 482-3125
  (800) 356-9315 book orders
  upperacces@aol.com
  Fulfillment services and retail distribution for small presses. Upper Access publishes catalog, *Big Books from Small Presses.*

- Intrepid Group, Inc.
  1331 Red Cedar Cr.
  Fort Collins, CO 80524
  (970) 493-3793
  fax (970) 493-8781
  Has free Publisher's Idea Kit.

- BookCrafters
  140 Buchanan
  Chelsea, MI 48118
  (313) 475-9145
  fax (313) 475-8591
  Also a Pick 'n Pack shipper and a book manufacturer.

## Publishers and booksellers associations

☑Denotes associations that sponsor trade shows.

- National Association of Independent Publishers
  Betsy Lampé
  P.O. Box 430
  Highland City, FL 33846-0430
  (941) 648-4420 (phone and fax)
  NAIP@aol.com
  Excellent, informative bimonthly newsletter, national book contest, networking and encouragement for authors. Co-op booths at trade shows among other benefits.

- Chesapeake Regional Area Booksellers
  11 Sparrow Valley Ct.
  Montgomery Village, MD 20879
  (301) 840-9074

- Florida Publishers Association
  Membership information
  P.O. Box 430
  Highland City, FL 33846-0430
  (941) 647-5951 (phone and fax)
  NAIP@aol.com
  www.gate.net/~fpabooks
  Offers newsletter for publishers and book promotion services. Biannual education seminars with top speakers. Web site for members. Co-op exhibits.

- Great Lakes Booksellers Association
  726 Columbus
  Grand Haven, MI 49417
  (616) 847-2460
  fax (616) 842-0051

- Houston Area Booksellers Association
  c/o Rhona Richardson
  Body, Mind, and Soul Books
  4386 Westheimer Ave.
  Houston, TX 77027
  (713) 729-8400
  fax (713) 726-0241

- ☑Intermountain Independent Booksellers Association
  1511 S. 1500 E.
  Salt Lake City, UT 84105
  (801) 484-9100; (800) 658-7928
  fax (801) 484-1595

- ☑Mid-Atlantic Booksellers Association
  108 S. 13th St.
  Philadelphia, PA 19107
  (215) 735-9598; (800) 480-7253
  fax (215) 735-2670

- ☑Mid-South Booksellers Association
  600 Frenchmen St.
  New Orleans, LA 70116
  (504) 943-9875 (phone/fax)
  Louisiana, Texas, Arkansas, Oklahoma, Mississippi and Western Tennessee

- New York/New Jersey Booksellers Association
  397 Arbuckle Ave.
  Cedarhurst, NY 11516
  (516) 295-1004

☑Mountains & Plains Booksellers
Association
805 La Porte Ave.
Fort Collins, CO 80521
(970) 484-5856
fax (970) 407-1479
(800) 752-0249
Colorado, Wyoming, New Mexico,
and Arizona. Excellent directory
may be purchased.

☑New England Booksellers
Association
847 Massachusetts Ave.
Cambridge, MA 02139
(800) 466-8711
(617) 576-3070
fax (617) 576-3091

☑Northern California Independent
Booksellers Assc.
5643 Paradise Drive, Suite 12
Corte Madera, CA 94925-1815
(415) 927-3937
fax (415) 927-3971

• Oklahoma Independent
Booksellers Association
10505 N. May
Oklahoma City, OK 73120
(405) 755-0020

☑Pacific Northwest Booksellers
Association
1510 Mill Street
Eugene, OR 97401
(541) 683-4363
fax (541) 683-3910

• San Diego Booksellers Association
c/o Adams Ave. Books
3502 Adams Ave.
San Diego, CA 92116
(619) 281-3330
fax (619) 281-0683
adamsave@adnc.com

• South-Central Booksellers
Association
Memphis State University Books
University Center
Memphis, TN 38152
(901) 678-2011
fax (901) 678-2665

• New Age Publishing & Retailing
Alliance
P.O. Box 9
6 Eastsound Square
Eastsound, WA 98245
(800) 297-9596
fax (360) 376-2704
napra@pacificrim.net

☑Southeast Booksellers Association
2730 Devine Street
Columbia, SC 29205
(800) 331-9617
fax (803) 252-8589
North Carolina, South Carolina,
Georgia, Alabama, Florida,
Mississippi, Tennessee.

• Southern California Booksellers
Association
P.O. Box 4176
Culver City, CA 90231-4178
(310) 476-6263
fax (310) 471-0399

☑Upper Midwest Booksellers
Association
4018 W. 65th St.
Edina, MN 55435
(612) 926-4102
fax (612) 926-6657
umbaoffice@aol.com

- Midwest Independent Publishers
Association
P.O. Box 580428
Minneapolis, MN 55458-0428
(612) 646-0475
fax (612) 521-0757
Paul Druckman
73243.2012@compuserve.com

- Mid-America Publisher's
Association
P.O. Box 30242
Lincoln, NE 68503-0242
(402) 421-9666
fax (402) 421-9093
Has a number of local chapters. Co-
op exhibits, book awards, and
conferences.

- Publishers Association of the South
700 S. 28th St. Ste 206
Birmingham, AL 35343
(205) 322-4579
fax (205) 326-1012
Excellent newsletter

- Publishers Marketing Association
2401 Pacific Coast Highway,
Suite 102
Hermosa Beach, CA 90254
(310) 372-2732
fax (310) 374-3342
PMAOnline@aol.com

- BookExpo America
828 S. Broadway
Tarrytown, NY 10591
(800) 637-0037; (914) 591-2665
fax (914) 591-2720
Formerly the American Booksellers
Association (ABA).

- Small Publishers Association of
North America (SPAN)
Marilyn and Tom Ross
P.O. Box 1306
Buena Vista, CO 81211-1306
(719) 395-4790
fax (719) 395-8374
SPAN@span-assn.org
SPAN membership includes an
information-packed newsletter; an
annual conference; a savings on
freight; access to merchant status
for credit cards; various discounts.

- Association of American
Publishers, Inc.
71 Fifth Avenue
New York, NY 10003-3004
(212) 255-0200
fax (212) 255-7007
Trade show, newsletters,
information.

### Radio and television interviews/ media promotions

- Pacesetter Publications
  Box 101330
  Denver, Co. 80250
  (800) 945-2488
  fax (303) 733-8288
  talkshows@aol.com
  Successful self-publisher Joe Sabah can tell you how to get on radio talk shows all across America without leaving your home. Contact him for his book and kit. Mention *Smart Self-Publishing* for a $10 discount!

- *Radio and TV Interview Reports*
  Bradley Communications Corp.
  135 E. Plumstead
  Lansdowne, PA 19050
  (610) 259-1070; (800) 989-1400
  fax (610) 284-3704
  A source of ideas for interviewers and producers.

- Planned Television Arts, Ltd.
  David Thalberg, vice-president
  301 E. 57th St.
  New York, NY 10022
  (212) 921-5111; (212) 715-1666
  A media placement and book publicity service. Publicists in daily contact with producers from major television talk shows.

- Book and Author Alert
  John Kremer
  Open Horizons
  209 S. Main St.,
  P.O. Box 205,
  Fairfield, IA 52556
  (800) 796-6130
  A mailing by John Kremer of selected titles to 1,500 media contacts per month. Three levels of contact available.

- Publishers News Service
  P.O. Box 20603
  Bradenton, FL 34203
  (941) 739-4801
  fax (941) 366-8309
  Each month PNS distributes camera-ready, feature-length newspaper articles and fillers to editors at 1,500 newspapers with a total circulation of nearly 100 million households. Nonfiction books eligible for service.

### Publicity

- Bartlett & Associates, Inc.
  8992 Edcliff Ct. SE
  Aumsville, OR 97325
  (503) 581-4155
  fax (503) 581-8742
  nelsonak@open.org
  In addition to doing publicity for authors, Bartlett has published, Publicity, a step-by-step guide for successful publicity campaigns. $9.50 includes shipping and handling.

- Event Management Services
  519 Cleveland St. Ste. 205
  Clearwater, FL 34615
  (813) 443-7115
  fax (813) 443-0835
  Pay only for interviews booked.
  Guarantees interviews with top
  radio, TV and newspapers. Free
  brochure. Publishes *Media Talk*
  magazine.

- Advocate Media Group
  212 E. Third Street
  Rome, GA 30161
  (706) 234-1566
  fax (716) 234-1252
  INTERVIEW1@aol.com
  Christian Media Specialists. Sets up
  interviews on radio and TV.
  Publishes *Interviews & Reviews*
  magazine.

- Publishers Media Service
  P.O. Box 20603
  Bradenton, FL 34203
  (941) 739-4801
  fax (941) 366-8309
  Provides public relations,
  advertising and marketing.

## Speakers organizations

- National Speakers Association
  1500 S. Priest Drive
  Tempe, AZ 85281
  (602) 968-2552
  fax (602) 968-0911
  www.nsaspeakers.org
  NSAmain@aol.com

- Speakers Unlimited
  Mike Frank, CSP, CPAE
  Box 27225
  Columbus, OH 43227
  (614) 864-3703
  fax (614) 864-3876
  Publisher of *For Professional
  Speakers Only,* a must-read for
  authors who want to work with
  speakers bureaus. Available only
  through Mike Frank. $24.95

- Washington Speakers Bureau
  1663 Prince St.
  Alexandria, VA 22314
  (703) 684-0555
  fax (703) 684-9132

## Some national media resources

- ABC's Good Morning America
  147 Columbus Ave.
  New York, NY 10023
  (212) 456-5900
  fax (212) 456-5962
  gma@abc.com

- Oprah Winfrey
  Box 909715
  Chicago, IL 60690
  (312) 633-0808
  fax (312) 633-1515
  Oprah has a recommended
  reading list.

- The Today Show
  30 Rockefeller Plaza, #304
  New York, NY 10112
  (212) 664-4602

- Ann Landers
  Creators Syndicate
  5777 W. Century Blvd. #700
  Los Angeles, CA 90045
  (310) 337-7003
  fax (310) 337-7625
  cre8ors@aol.com

- Associated Press Broadcast
  Services
  1825 K. Street, NW #710
  Washington, D.C. 20006
  (202) 736-1100; (800) 821-4747
  fax (202) 736-1199
- United Press International
  1400 Eye Street, 8th Floor
  Washington, DC 20005
  (202) 898-8000
  fax (202) 898-8057
- National Public Radio
  635 Massachusetts Ave. NW
  Washington, DC 20001-3753
  NPRLIST@npr.org
  E-mail for list of all NPR program
  address. Write for guidelines for
  submitting ideas for shows such as
  "All Things Considered."

## Indexing

- Municipal Code Corporation
  P.O. Box 2235
  Tallahassee, FL 32316
  (800) 262-2633
  fax (904) 575-8852
  lawton@municode.com
  www.municode.com
- Hazel Blumberg-McKee
  13418 N. Meridian Road
  Tallahassee, FL 32312
  (904) 893-7557
  hazelcb@spolaris.net

## Credentials:

### Bar codes

Note: Adhesive bar code labels for application to already-printed books are available from either Aaron Graphics or Fotel/GGX. Some book manufacturers and cover designers now are capable of generating bar codes.

- Fotel/GGX Associates
  6 Grace Avenue
  Great Neck, NY 11021
  (800) 834-8088
  fax (516) 487-6449
- Precision Photography, Inc.
  1150 North Tustin Ave.
  Anaheim, CA 92807
  (800) 872-9977; (714) 632-9000
  fax (714) 630-6581
- Aaron Graphics
  2903 Saturn St. Unit G
  Brea, CA 92821
  (714) 985-1290; (800) 345-8944
  fax (714) 985-1295

## ISBN

- R. R. Bowker/ISBN/Advanced
  Books Information
  Diana Fumando, manager
  121 Chanlon Road
  New Providence, NJ 07974
  (800) 521-8110; (908) 665-6770
  fax (908) 665-6749

## Library of Congress Catalog Card Number

- For Preassigned Card Number:
  Library of Congress
  Cataloging in Publication Div.
  Washington, D.C. 20540
  Attn: Preassigned Card Number
  Program

- For Cataloging in Publication:
  Library of Congress
  Cataloging in Publication Div.
  Washington, D.C. 20540
  Attn: CIP Program
  (202) 707-9812

## Copyright

- Register of Copyrights
  Library of Congress
  Washington, D.C. 20559

## Book manufacturers

- BookCrafters
  140 Buchanan
  Chelsea, MI 48118
  (313) 475-9145
  fax (313) 475-8591
  Sheet-fed and web presses. Also does fulfillment and Pick 'n Pack shipping. Ask for copy of *Get Ready, Get Set, Go!* Instructions for customers on preparing book for printing and binding.

- Braun-Brumfield, Inc.
  P.O. Box 1203
  100 N. Staebler Rd.
  Ann Arbor, MI 48106
  (313) 662-3291
  fax (313) 662-1667
  Web and sheet-fed presses. Offers informative, free, *Book Manufacturing Glossary.*

- RR Donnelley & Sons Company
  109 Westpark Drive, Ste. 480
  Brentwood, TN 37027-5032
  (615) 371-2113
  fax (615) 371-2115
  Sheet-fed and web presses. One of the largest printing houses in the world.

- Gilliland Printing
  215 North Summit
  Arkansas City, KS 67005
  (316) 442-0500; (800) 332-8200
  fax (316) 442-8504
  Sheet-fed presses. Usually fast turnaround.

- McNaughton & Gunn, Inc.
  960 Woodland Dr.
  Saline, MI 48176-0010
  (313) 429-5411
  fax (800) 677-2665
  Sheet-fed presses.

- Thomson-Shore, Inc.
  7300 Joy Road
  Dexter, MI 48130-0305
  (313) 426-3939
  fax (800) 706-4545
  www.tshore.com
  Sheet-fed press. Publishes free
  informative newsletter. Call to be
  put on list.

- Walsworth Publishing Co.
  306 N. Kansas Ave.
  Marceline, MO 64658
  (800) 369-2646, (816) 376-3543
  fax (816) 258-7798
  www.walsworth.com
  Sheet-fed, small- to-medium press
  runs, less than 10,000 copies.

- C.J. Krehbiel Co.
  3962 Virginia Ave.
  Cincinnati, OH 45227
  (800) 598-7808
  fax (513) 271-6082
  Web press (long runs, 10,000 copies
  or more).

- United Graphics
  2916 Marshall Ave.
  P.O. Box 559
  Mattoon, IL 61938
  (217) 235-7161
  fax (217) 234-6274
  Sheet-fed, short to medium runs.

- Victor Graphics
  1211 Bernard Drive
  Baltimore, MD 21223
  (410) 233-8300
  fax (410) 233-8304
  pineapple@victorgraphics.com
  Sheet-fed and web presses.

**Cover designers**

Note: Many cover designers also
design Web pages. See Appendix
C for more Web page information.

- Pearl and Associates
  One South Ocean Blvd.,
  Suite 312
  Boca Raton, FL 33432
  (561) 338-0380
  fax (561) 338-9460
  75300.2231@compuserve.com

- Tracy Hall Art and Design
  7571 Kirkwood Drive
  West Chester, OH 45069
  (513) 755-2308 (phone/fax)

- Paul DesJardien
  907 9th St.
  Mukilteo, WA 98275
  (206) 287-8155
  des@seanet.com

- Lightbourne Images
  Bram and Gaelyn Larrick
  2565 Siksiyou Blvd., Suite 1G
  Ashland, OR 97520
  (800) 697-9833
  fax (541) 482-1730
  waking@opendoor.com
  www.waking.com/lightbourne

- Cheryl Nathan
  Cover design and illustration
  9495 Evergreen Pl. #406
  Ft. Lauderdale, FL 33324
  (305) 476-7819

- Robert Howard Graphic Design
  631 Mansfield Dr.
  Fort Collins, CO 80525
  (970) 225-0083 (phone/fax)

- Tantillo Design Group
  8 Laurel Park
  Wappingers Falls, NY 12590
  (914) 462-1071
  fax (914) 462-1626
  shawangunk@mhv.net

## Illustrations/graphic design

- Don Doyle
  Eight Damon St.
  North Reading, MA 08164
  (508) 664-6353
  A commercial artist with
  experience in calligraphy, fine art
  and design. Has done book
  illustrations.

- Christopher Grotke
  c/o Tabby House
  4429 Shady Lane
  Charlotte Harbor, FL 33980
  (941) 629-7646
  fax (941) 629-4270
  tabbyhouse@helbing.net
  www.tabbyhouse.com
  Illustrations, designs, cartoons.
  Nominated for Caldecott Award.
  Has illustrated several books,
  including this one.

- Amy Sorvaag Lindman
  200 S. Cedar Loop
  Colville, WA 99114
  Book illustrations.

- Tracy Hall Art and Design
  See entry under cover designers.

- Diane Getson
  3431 Clark Road, #232
  Sarasota, FL 34231
  (941) 923-9743

## Typesetting

- B&C Typesetting
  Bob Lefebvre, manager
  10245 Chadwick Ave.
  Englewood, FL 34224
  (941) 475-2130
  fax/modem (941) 474-2903

## Book repairs

- Dunn & Company, Inc.
  David Dunn, president
  75 Green St.
  Clinton, MA 01510-0968
  (508) 368-8505
  fax (508) 368-7867

## Bound galleys

- Graphic Illusions (formerly Crane Duplicating)
  17 Shad Hole Road
  Dennisport, MA 02639
  (508) 760-1601
  fax (508) 760-1544

- PLC Inc.
  23 Alabama Ave.
  Island Park, NY 11558
  (800) 431-1131
  fax (516) 897-7267
  Also does very short press runs, as low as 50 or 100 copies. Call for price sheet.

## Packing materials/shipping supplies

- Uline
  950 Albrecht Drive
  Lake Bluff, IL 60044
  1-800-295-5510

## Commission reps/publishers reps

- The National Association of Independent Publishers Representatives
  111 East 14th Street
  Zechendorf Towers, Suite 157
  New York, NY 10003
  (508) 877-5328
  fax (508) 788-0208
  naipr@aol.com
  Free marketing material and directory of publishers representatives (also known as commission reps) that belong to association.

- Booklink
  Terry A. Hicks
  132-A 3rd Ave. East
  Hendersonville, NC 28792
  (704) 693-9528
  fax (704) 697-6377

- George Scheer Associates
  Deborah Donnell
  3814 Walker Ave.
  Greensboro, NC 27403
  (800) 265-8504
  fax (910) 854-6908

- Hopkins Group
  Eileen Hopkins
  325 Lauderdale Rd.
  Nashville, TN 37205
  (615) 385-0703
  fax (615) 292-4587
  ekhopkins@aol.com

- Monahan Associates
  Kevin Monahan
  604 Boothe Hill Road
  Chapel Hill, NC 27514
  (919) 933-7879
  fax (919) 929-0562
  kvmon@msn.com

- Morris & Assoc.
  Gary Morris
  2300 Hazelwood Lane
  Clearwater, FL 34623
  (813) 726-8834
  fax (813) 726-0195

- Roghaar Associates
  Linda Roghaar
  2809 Azalea Place
  Nashville, TN 37204
  (615) 269-8977; (800) 446-4095
  fax (615) 297-6630

### Bookstore chains

You need publishing credentials plus an arrangement with a wholesaler or distributor to be considered by a chain. Some chains are easier to deal with than others. If you have a regional topic, begin with a regional buyer.

- Barnes & Noble/B. Dalton Bookseller
  Small Press Department
  122 Fifth Ave.
  New York, NY 10011
  (212) 633-3300

- Books-A-Million
  402 Industrial Lane
  Birmingham, AL 35211
  (205) 942-3737
  fax (205) 945-1772

- Walden Book Company/Borders Group Inc.
  Small Press Department
  311 Maynard St.
  Ann Arbor, MI 48104
  (313) 913-1100

### Book clubs

- Book-of-the-Month Club
  1271 Avenue of the Americas
  New York, NY 10020-2686
  (212) 522-4200

- Quality Paperback Book Club
  1271 Avenue of the Americas
  New York, NY 10020
  (212) 522-4200

### Instore book displays

- ABELexpress
  230 East Main St.
  Carnegie, PA 15106
  (800) 542-9001
  fax (412) 279-5012
  Floor and counter displays; shipping cartons.

- City Diecutting, Inc.
  2 Babcock Place,
  West Orange, NJ 07052
  (201)736-1224
  fax (201) 736-1248

- Traverse Bay Display Co.
  4366 Deerwood Road
  Traverse City, MI 49686
  (800 ) 240-9802
  fax (616) 938-3296

## Remainders

- Camex International, Inc.
  535 Fifth Avenue
  New York, NY 10017
  (212) 682-8400

- The Texas Bookman
  8650 Denton Drive
  Dallas, TX 75235
  (214) 350-6648
  fax (214) 352-0726

- JLM Remainders
  2370 East Little Creek Road
  Norfolk, VA 23518
  (804) 627-4160
  fax (804) 587-7421

- Book Country
  503 Rodi Road
  Pittsburgh, PA 15235
  (412) 242-4000
  fax (412) 243-5114

- Fairmount Books, Inc.
  2316 Delaware Ave., Suite 454
  Buffalo, NY 14216-2687
  (905) 475-0988
  fax (905) 475-1072

## Editors and editing services

Negotiate a per-page or per-project price, rather than hourly rate. Clarify nature of services in advance. Ask for references or samples of work.

- Chester Baum
  P.O. Box 71
  Oxford, MD 21654
  (410) 226-5907

- Nancy Koesy Parker
  2530 E. North Street, Ste 6A
  Greenville, SC 29615
  (864) 322-5594
  fax (864) 322-5596
  NKPediting@aol.com

- Abigail Grotke
  c/o Tabby House
  4429 Shady Lane
  Charlotte Harbor, FL 33980
  (941) 629-7646
  tabbyhouse@helbing.net

- Heyward (Hank) Hawkins
  550 Wedge Lane
  Longboat Key, FL 34228
  (941) 383-7622 (phone/fax)

- PMC Communications
  P.O. Box 1948
  Fair Oaks, CA 95628
  (916) 863-5326
  fax (916) 966-9675

- Nancy Wettlaufer
  5335 Calle Florida
  Siesta Key, FL 34242
  (941) 349-8327
  wettlaufer@aol.com

- Beverly Horning Gore
  124 Baldwin Court
  Port Charlotte, FL 33952
  (941) 764-6558 Phone/fax

# Appendix C

## Building your own Web page

CREATING A WORLD WIDE WEB site is easier than you might think. More and more small businesses, including self-publishers and small presses, can now add their own Home page to the World Wide Web at little, or even no, extra cost over the basic monthly charge for their Internet Service Provider or online service. Many small publishers do not take advantage of this inexpensive marketing tool because they have assumed the page needed to be created by a professional computer artist and they feared that it would be expensive.

Good news! Creating a simple Home page doesn't require any "professional" programming at all. In fact, if you are computer literate enough to format a style sheet for your manuscript pages, you can learn the fundamentals of Web page construction and build a basic site, start to finish, in just a couple of hours. It will take more time to massage it and make it look more professional.

### Basic Web page construction

The World Wide Web is organized by "sites" and "pages." A single-page site, or the first page of a multi-page site, is called a Home page. It is usually an introduction to the site, with a menu that offers access to other pages in the site, if there are any. Each page can incorporate many different elements, including text and graphics as well as "links" to other spots on the Web. Those links can be to other parts of the same page, other pages in the same site, or even to other sites on the Web. In addition, advanced Web-page creators (called Webmasters) can incorporate E-mail, sound and even video clips in their Website.

Overall, a Web page is nothing but a text document done with a word processing or other program, with codes inserted to tell the Web browser software, such as *Netscape Navigator* or Microsoft *Explorer*, that is part of your Internet access package, how to display the page on the screen of a monitor.

Creating this type of document is very similar to formatting the pages of your manuscript—except that you are able to see only the typed document, not the formatted page, until you display it in the browser program. That makes Web page construction about like doing paint-by-numbers while wearing a blindfold, but peeking every once in a while.

The codes, called "tags," are part of worldwide standardized system called "Hypertext Markup Language," or HTML. Every tag in HTML begins with <, and they all end with >. The tags around the commands that tell the browser to start a particular format look like this: *<command>* and the ones that tell the browser to stop the format look like this: *</command>*. All HTML documents begin with <HTML> and end with </HTML>. The beginning and ending tags for a command are the same except for the forward slash. The programming is not case sensitive—HTML will be read the same as html. Also you need to know that the tags cannot overlap each other.

You must use the opposite philosophy of pantry stocking–not first in, first out, but last in, first out.

Then the file is saved to ASCII, "text only," using the file extension: html (Mac) or htm. (PC) HTML does not recognize other document file formats.

Here is a very basic document with simple HTML tags:

```
<HTML>
<HEAD><TITLE>Tabby House Home Page</TITLE></HEAD>
<BODY>
<P><H1=CENTER>Welcome to Tabby House's Home Page</H1>
<P><H2=CENTER>Award-Winning Book Packagers for Self-Publishing
Authors</H2>
<HR1>Tabby House, an award-winning book-packaging and publishing
company prides that itself on honesty, good service and an outstanding
product. Tabby House is the publisher of <I>Smart Self-Publishing: An
author's guide to producing a marketable book</I>, a book which is widely
read and well-respected by self-publishing authors nationwide.
</BODY>
</HTML>
```

To make your own HTML page, first know the basic commands and how and where to place them.

Let's go over the commands first, then we can see the page: <HTML> Begins a document in hypertext markup language. <HEAD > is the line at the top of the screen that tells you where you are, and <TITLE> is what it will say in that line. The <BODY> of the page begins with a large (indicated by the "1" after the H), centered headline, <H1>, that reads: Welcome to Tabby House's Home Page, followed by a smaller, centered sub head, <H2>, that reads: Award-Winning Book Packagers for Self-Publishing Authors. Finally, after a large horizontal rule, <HR1>, which includes a paragraph break, comes the text: Tabby House, an award-winning book-packaging and

publishing company prides itself on honesty, good service and an outstanding product. Tabby House is the publisher of <I>(begin italics)Smart Self-Publishing: An author's guide to producing a marketable book</I>(end italics),

a book which is widely read and well-respected by self-publishing authors nationwide.</BODY> (end body) and finally </HTML>(end document).

Here is how the coded page would appear on the browser:

| Netscape-[Tabby House Home Page] |
|---|
| Menu bar |
| Location: http://www.tabbyhouse.com/index |

# Welcome to Tabby House's Home Page
## Award-Winning Book Packagers for Self-Publishing Authors

---

Tabby House, an award-winning book-packaging and publishing company prides itself on honesty, good service and an outstanding product. Tabby House is the publisher of *Smart Self-Publishing: An author's guide to producing a marketable book*, a book which is widely read and well-respected by self-publishing authors nationwide.

That wasn't too hard, was it? Now, let's fancy up the page a bit, using a couple of slightly more advanced features. By the way, an excellent software program for building a Web page is *Web Page Creator*, by Steve Parker. (See Appendix A for details.)

### Adding graphics

Pictures and other graphics that you want to add to your page must be saved to separate files and referred to in the document in a way that the browser can find them. The graphic files must be in a format that the browser can read, either GIF (.gif) files or JPEG (.jpg) files. TIFF (.tif) files are too big and the format can't be read by the browsers. When you get to the spot that you want a graphic, for instance your imprint logo, inserted, simply type in <IMG SRC=*logo*.gif> where *logo* is the file name of your imprint. The browser program will find the file and retrieve and display the graphic. There are a host of commands that you can use to position the graphic and wrap your text but they are too numerous to go into here. Two good books to guide you are *HTML For the World Wide Web*, by Elizabeth Castro, and *Designing For The Web*, by Jennifer Neiderst. (See Appendix A.)

### Adding links

The feature that makes the World Wide Web so powerful is its capability to quickly link your site with other sites all over the world. You do this by inserting "clickable" links anywhere on your page that you feel they are desirable.

To create a link from your Home page to another page within your site you only need to type: <A HREF="file:///filename.htm">*text*</A> where *text* is the word or words you want to be highlighted as clickable. When that text is clicked the browser will locate the file and transfer the viewer to it. For instance, by typing the mention of our book in the simulated page above as <A HREF="file:///catalog.htm"><I>Smart Self-Publishing: An author's guide to producing a marketable book</I></A>, We would have created a clickable link between the book title and the catalog section of the Web site. Clicking the link would transport the viewer to the catalog page and ordering information.

To create a link from your Web page to an outside page you first need the address (called the URL) of the destination site. For instance, if you want to link your site to Tabby House's Web site, you would type: <A HREF="http://www.tabbyhouse.com/publish/"> Tabby House Web Site </A>, where "Tabby House Web Site" is the text you wanted to highlight as the clickable link.

Finally, if you want to provide a direct link to you or your office via E-mail you would type in: <A HREF="mailto:name@site.com">text</A>. Where *text* is again the text to be highlighted as a link. Our web site has: <A HREF="mailto: Publisher @TabbyHouse.com"> IMG SRC=tom.jpg</A> typed in. When a viewer clicks the link, a picture of our cat, Tom, an E-mail form pops up with our address and the sender's address already filled in. All the viewer has to do is type their message and click the button.

## Posting your page

After you have created your page you will want to transfer it to the appropriate spot on a Web server so the world can find it. A server is the computer that is maintained by your Internet Service Provider or online service, and is connected to the Internet. Contact your provider and you will be given (or rented) a subdirectory on the server, which will hold all the files that make up your Web site, and instructions on how to get the files to your provider, by either uploading them or on disk.

Once you have placed your page on the Internet you will still be able to modify it if you wish to. Be sure your server registers your site with lots of search programs, and under as many cross-referencing headings as you think necessary, so you will be easily found. You might, for instance, list your book under: publisher name, subject, title, your last name, genre (poetry, sci-fi, mystery), or even the titles of poems or key locations where the story action takes place, if you think that might attract attention.

We are pleased to give credit to Sprint for allowing us to use an article from their newsletter, *Sound Advice*, Summer 1996, as the guide for this appendix. Sprint's article was so well-written and easy to follow that we called for permission, which they generously gave. We have altered the text a bit to personalize it, and replaced their graphics with our own.

# Appendix D

**Ask editor Chester Baum**

**Q.** How long is a "short story," and how long should a book of short stories be?
**A.** A short story runs anywhere from five thousand to ten thousand words. Most modern collections contain about a dozen of them.

**Q.** How long should a novel be?
**A.** There is no high end for self-publishers except the limit imposed by budget. Willa Cather's novel, *Shadows on the Rock*, is 78,400 words, representing the low end of the scale. Tolstoy's *War and Peace* is more than 600,000 words. Obviously there is a happy medium, but you don't want to publish something so skinny that there is no room on the spine for a title.

Large publishing companies are publishing virtually no new authors of fiction, so standards that might be employed by their manuscript readers to determine just the right combination of literary worth and popular appeal that would justify publishing a novel are largely irrelevant to the self-publishing author.

**Q.** What about a book of poetry?
**A.** It took all of Shakespeare's 154 sonnets (exclusive of notes and appendixes) to fill up the 77 pages that comprise the slim volume

published by Yale University Press. I have seen collections of individual's poetry that number several hundred pages, and many fine collections that are fewer than one hundred pages.

If you are uncertain which poems to include in your book ask for editorial assistance from your book packager.

**Q.** Please recommend a reference book that I can use to help me with my work in process.
**A.** Those of you who have a work in process in any genre may find it helpful, before rushing into publication, to read some analyses of literature that have been accepted as excellent. Many college textbooks might help you, but the one which has the advantage of comment by an often published and critically acclaimed novelist and poet (along with the insights of academicians) is Brooks, Purser and Warren, *Approach to Literature*, 5th edition, 1975.

Books such as this should not discourage you. Examples of some of the best fiction and poetry in our language should help you learn what the elements of good writing are and discover that those elements exist in your own work.

My remarks about increasing your literary background apply more to the first-time writer than to those experienced writers who know that their work already compares favorably to published fiction or poetry.

*Chester Baum, book and manuscript editor, is the retired chairman of the English Department at St. Andrew's School, Middletown, Delaware.*

# Glossary

**—A—**

**Acid-free paper:** Neutral pH paper or alkaline paper, free from acid or other ingredients that destroy paper. Some libraries prefer acid-free paper, but it costs more. It's good for archival works and family histories—books that last and don't circulate much.

**Advance copies:** Copies of book sent to a customer right after it comes off press but before the rest of the run is shipped.

**Air:** White space. This is the extra space between lines, margins or around art work to keep the page from looking too crowded, or dark.

**Align/alignment:** To line up or position the print on a page with that on the adjacent pages and on the reverse of the same page.

**Appendix:** Material in the back of the book which is related but not essential. Part of the "back matter." See *The Chicago Manual of Style* for how to set up the appendix and other parts of your book.

**Art/artwork:** Illustrations, photographs, drawings, paintings, and maps.

**Author alterations (A.A.):** These are changes made by the author during blueline proofing and are charged to the author/publisher.

**Author/publisher:** A self-publishing author who has applied for a bank of ISBNs and either set up the book himself or employed a packager to do the project.

# —B—

**Back lining:** A strip of paper or fabric used to strengthen the spine of a casebound book.

**Back flap:** The back inside fold of a dust jacket, usually featuring a photo and biographical information of the author, and publisher's imprint.

**Back matter:** The selections at the back of the book including appendix, glossary, index and bibliography, and related material.

**Bad break:** Starting or ending a page with a widow or orphan or other awkward or messy look. May also refer to an inappropriate hyphenation in a word at the end of a line.

**Bar code:** A series of vertical bars encoded with the title, ISBN, and price of your book. Bookland EAN bar code should be printed at bottom of back cover.

**Binder board:** A stiff, high-grade composition board used in book binding. The cloth is glued over it to make the case or hard cover.

**Bleed:** An image or color that extends beyond the trim edge of the page, or from one page to another in a spread. Most book covers are designed to bleed, rather than have a border at the trim edge.

**Bluelines (blues):** Bluelines, like architectural drawings, are a photoprint made from stripped-up negatives or positives, used to check the position of the elements, and assuring that the pages are in order. They should not be used for a final proofing. Bluelines must be approved and returned quickly to keep book production on schedule.

**Body copy:** The primary part of the text.

**Body text:** Type used for the body copy. It may be different from that used for headings.

**Boldface:** The glossary words are set in **boldface** (b.f.) or a heavier face type to make them stand out.

**Book block:** The sewn and trimmed signatures which are ready to be bound. Everything put together but the cover.

**Book cloth:** The special cloth used for book covers. Like linens, the quality is determined by the number of threads per inch and their strength.

**Book manufacturing:** The specialized process of printing and binding the book.

**Book packaging:** A process by which a self-publishing author contracts to have a book professionally produced, receiving the entire press run.

**Book style:** Adhering to an accepted set of standard abbreviations, spellings, capitalizations and punctuation. Use *The Chicago Manual of Style, The Associated Press Stylebook,* and dictionary.

**Bound galley:** A copy of the finished book, uncorrected page proofs, or manuscript bound with a cheap cover and sent to those reviewers who want to see the book in advance of publication. Sometimes called "Cranes" after the company that originally produced them.

**Browser:** A software package such as *Netscape* or Microsoft *Explorer* that guides the user through the World Wide Web and displays HTML codes as text and graphics.

**Bulk:** The thickness of a book without the cover. Heavier papers can "bulk" up a book to make it thicker, sometimes important for thin volumes that must be a certain thickness if they are to be casebound.

**—C—**

**C1S:** Coated one side. Papers used for paperback book covers and dust jackets have an enamel coating on one side.

**C2S:** Coated two sides. Both sides of the paper used for paperback book covers are coated with enamel.

**Camera-ready copy:** An often misused term meaning the material ready for reproduction—the final copy going to the book manufacturer.

**Casebound:** Another name for hardcover.

**Cataloging in Publication/CIP:** Information for catalog card provided by the Library of Congress (after its review of the manuscript) or by some library distributors for inclusion on the copyright page.

**Coated paper:** Mineral and chemical substances, usually called enamel, that are applied to the paper to produce greater opacity or brightness. Can be either glossy or matte finish.

**Coffee-table book:** Large book with many illustrations, often with color photographs or prints, which is used for display.

**Color key:** An overlay proof composed of an individual colored acetate sheet for each of the PMS colors used by the printer, used to check register, obvious blemishes and size.

**Color proof:** A laser proof showing the approximate colors of the cover or artwork. Used to check for register or errors.

**Copyright:** Ownership of the work, protected by law. Copyright should be in name of owner—the author, publisher or whoever paid for work.

**Corner marks:** Open parts of squares placed on original copy as a positioning guide. Shows the actual size of your book pages. Sometimes known as crop marks or printer's marks.

**Crop/crop marks:** To crop is to eliminate a part of a photograph or other illustration. Crop marks show the area to be saved, or to be eliminated.

**Customer service rep (CSR):** The service representative at the book manufacturer who is assigned to each project. Good reps will shepherd you and the book through the printing and binding process, facilitating production and schedules.

## —D—

**DPI:** Dots per inch. The more dpi, the sharper the reproduction. Books should be printed at no less, and preferably more than 600 dpi for good quality reproduction. Most laser printers output only at 300 dpi.

**Distributor:** The middleman between the publisher and the retail outlet.

**Drop ship**: To ship an order to one address, and bill charges to another.

**Duotone:** A two-color halftone reproduction from a one-color original.

**Dust jacket:** The printed paper cover wrapped around a casebound book. Also called a book jacket

## —E—

**E-mail:** Mail or messages sent electronically using the Internet. You need to be connected through a server before you can connect to others. An excellent method of keeping networking contacts alive.

**EAN Bookland bar code:** A series of vertical lines printed on the book's cover or jacket. The lines are encoded with price, ISBN, and title, and are scanned by computers for inventory and sales records.

**Editor:** Someone born with a red pen in hand who will help you breathe life into your material, assist with style and check for accuracy.

**EM dash or space:** EM is a unit of measure in typesetting equal to the point size of the type in question. An em dash — is always used instead of a double hyphen -- to indicate a change of thought in a sentence. There should be no space between the em dash and adjacent letters.

**EN dash or space:** Half the size of an em. Used instead of a hyphen to indicate range of dates or numbers, i.e. 1910–14.

**Endsheets:** Two pages of strong paper wrapped around the book block of a casebound book, with one leaf of each pasted to the inside board of the case. Can be plain or printed with colors and designs.

**Extract:** Section of material taken from another book or from another author, set in smaller type or indented.

## —F—

**Fax:** An inexpensive and speedy electronic means to send printed or written information, receive orders and communicate via telephone circuits.

**F&G:** Folded and gathered, not yet bound book block.

**Facing pages:** Two pages that face each other when the book is open.

**Film lamination:** A process of bonding plastic film on the cover to protect it from scratching and improve the appearance.

**Font:** Full assortment (upper and lower case, numerals, symbols, etc.) of a specific size and style of type.

**Foreword:** A statement by an expert, (not the author) in the front matter. Do not confuse with "forward," which means to advance or move ahead.

**Front flap:** Usually features a synopsis or teaser about the content, the price, and ISBN.

**Front matter:** The front section (foreword, preface, introduction, etc.), with pages numbered in Roman numerals, that comes before the book body.

**Fulfillment house:** A place where orders, usually for single copies, are taken and books shipped. Will have credit card capability and will take 800 calls twenty-four hours.

**—G—**

**Galley/galley proof:** Typeset material before it has been formatted into book form.

**Gutter:** The blank space between columns of type or text and spine.

**Gray scale:** A scale of gradations of gray, from white to black. It measures the range and contrast of a scanned image.

## —H—

**Half-title page:** The page in the front matter containing only the book title or section title, it precedes the title page and is often used as the "autographing page."

**Hard copy:** The paper printout of what is on your computer screen.

**Halftone:** A photographic image that has been printed through a screen composed of minute dots. This breaks up the image so that it can be reproduced with proper contrast in the printing process.

**Header:** The headline at the beginning of a chapter (chapter head) or the beginning of a section (section head) or a new topic (subhead).

**High contrast:** The darkness between adjoining areas is well-defined, sometimes greater than in the original photograph.

**Home page:** The index or menu page of a Web site. The page that a user will be taken to first, and from which they can get to all parts of the Web site.

**HTML:** HyperText Markup Language. The coding language used to program Web sites.

## —I—

**Imprint:** The identifying name of the publishing company, which is printed on the book.

**Independent publisher:** A publishing house which is not publicly owned or one of the "Big Guys."

**International Standard Book Number:** A number assigned to the publisher by R.R. Bowker that identifies each book. The ISBN should be printed on the copyright page, the back cover and spine.

**Internet:** A system of worldwide communication over telephone lines and satellite links which is available through Internet providers (usually local) or Online services such as AmericaOnline or CompuServe.

**ISBN:** See International Standard Book Number.

**Italic:** Sloped letters. If needed for emphasis, *use sparingly!* Also used to mark titles of books and magazines in text.

## —J—

**Justify:** To have the text set flush left and/or right. The lines of text are squared off and the type is spaced to evenly fill the line. Most books are justified. This one, however, is justified on the left margin, but not the right.

## —K—

**Kerning:** Adjusting the space between two characters for aesthetics, so they appear closer together, or farther apart. This word, fly, is not kerned. This one is: fly. Note the spaces between the "f" and the "l."

## —L—

**Layout:** A working diagram of how the page(s) will look for artist, typesetter, or printer to follow as a guide.

**Leaders:**............Rows of dots or dashes to guide the eye across the page. Use sparingly. Try to avoid using them in the table of contents.

**Leading:** The space between lines of type, measured from baseline to baseline and expressed in points.

**Leaf:** Each piece of paper in the book, with a page on each side.

**Library binding:** A stronger, heavily reinforced binding that meets the standards of the American Library Association.

**Link(s):** Hyperlinks. Those coded and highlighted words or icons in an HTML document that, when clicked, will transport a Web user to another page in a Web site or even to another site in the Web.

**Long run:** A print run in excess of 10,000 copies.

**—M—**

**Marketing:** Finding out what the public wants and meeting its needs. A self-publishing author's responsibility.

**Mass market paperback:** Books produced inexpensively for distribution in supermarkets, drug stores and some bookstores. Usually small, approximately 4½ x 6 inches, and produced in quantity at low unit cost.

**Match print:** A photographic print of a four-color cover or page made from the film that the plates will be made from. Used by the pressman to check accuracy of the colors as they are printed.

**Matte:** Dull finish. No luster or gloss.

**Mechanicals:** Copy that uses overlays to indicate the position and register of each element or color to be printed. Color key.

**Moisture content:** A measure of relative humidity that expresses the amount of water in paper.

**—N—**

**NAIP:** National Association of Independent Publishers.

**NAIPR:** National Association of Independent Publishers Representatives.

**Nocurl paper:** A new process that keeps paper book covers from curling up in high humidity.

**—O—**

**Offset lithography:** A printing process in which image area and non-image area exist on same plate and are separated by chemical repulsion.

**Orphan:** The first line of a paragraph that is left at the bottom of a page. Orphans signal lack of professionalism in book formatting.

**Otabind™:** One of several patented binding processes that adapt perfect binding so that it can lie flat without being held open.

**Out of register:** Pages on both sides of sheet or colors that are not aligned.

**—P—**

**Printer's error (P.E.):** A necessary correction or change caused by an error by the printer or typesetter and is not billed to the customer.

**PPI (pages per inch):** The number of pages contained in one inch stack of paper. Varies depending on the weight of the paper.

**Page:** One side of a leaf.

**Page proof:** Proof of type in page form. The final proofs before going to camera-ready.

**Paperbound:** Paperback or softcover book.

**Perfect bound**: A binding method which uses flexible adhesive to hold each page in place after folds along the spine have been cut off. Most paperback books are perfect bound.

**Pick 'n Pack:** A shipping house that will store and ship your books. You fax them your orders and they will pick, pack and ship them for you. Some also have fulfillment services.

**Plastic comb binding:** Also called spiral or GBC binding. A type of binding made of rolled, rigid plastic cut in the shape of a comb or rake, and inserted through slots punched in the spine edge of the book pages. Cookbooks and workbooks are often bound this way.

**Preface:** Part of front matter and serves as introductory material.

**Prelims:** Preliminary pages or front matter.

**Prepress:** All the manufacturing setup work prior to going on the press.

**Process colors:** Yellow, cyan blue, magenta red and black. Thousands of colors can be produced using these colors in various combinations.

**Publisher:** The company or person whose ISBN is applied to the book, whose imprint appears on the title page, and who presents the literary product to the public.

**Publishers rep:** A person who tries to sell your book to a distributor, wholesaler, or to the independent stores. See commission rep.

## —Q—

**Questions about book packaging:** Call Tabby House for free consultation anytime during business hours (EST), (941) 629-7646, or E-mail Publisher@TabbyHouse.com.

## —R—

**Ragged right:** Type that is justified on the left margin and is unjustified on the right. This book's type is set ragged right.

**Resolution:** The degree of sharpness in either a screen display or an image, measured in dots per inch. A low resolution (72 dpi) is used in newspaper printing and for computer screen images, while higher resolutions (300 or 600 dpi) are used in laser printers. Highest resolution (1200 to 2450 dpi) comes from laser typesetters and image setters.

**Retail:** Selling to the general public at the stated price of the product.

**Recto:** A right-hand, odd-numbered page.

**Roman type:** A regular typeface, as opposed to italic or bold face versions of the same type.

**Rules:** Vertical or horizontal lines on a page.

**Run:** Press run. The number of copies printed and in a single printing.

**Running head:** A headline or chapter title repeated at the top of each page, for quick reference of the reader.

# —S—

**Saddlestitch:** A binding process that fastens the pages or signatures of a book together with wire stitches or staples through the middle fold.

**Sans serif:** A style of typeface that does not have serifs or ticks at the ends of letters. More difficult to read. Do not use for book text. However, sans serif can be used effectively for headers or subheads.

**Screen:** A network of crisscross lines of dots which break up a continuous tone image into a pattern that can be printed in black and white to represent gradations of grey. Without a screen your photographs will be reproduced as if by a copy machine. Used to make halftones.

**Self-publisher:** Realistic and courageous author who understands the reality of the publishing market, knows that a book is a product, and takes control of his or her destiny.

**Serifs:** Small extensions or "ticks" on the bases and tops of letters. They make the type easier to read because they lead the eye to the next letter. Serif fonts should be used for the body text of a book.

**Service bureau:** A company that specializes in support services for designers, printers and photographers. Service bureaus do screening, halftones, color separations, proofs and camera-ready output.

**Sheet-fed press:** A printing press that prints on individual sheets of paper. Each sheet is then folded and trimmed to make a signature. Most economical for short-run books.

**Shrink wrap:** A clear plastic covering, heat shrunk to fit tightly around copies of your book. Helps protect books during shipping and from humidity. Sometimes enhances salability.

**Signature:** A part of a book consisting a group of pages that has been folded and trimmed. There may be 4, 8, 16, 24, or 32 pages to the signature. Plan your book so that the page count comes out in even signatures.

**Small press:** An independent press. A small press can be a single-title author/publisher, or a rights-buying publisher.

**Smart self-publisher:** Someone who does it right!

**Smyth-sewn:** Signatures sewn together with thread by linked stitching on back of the fold and through the centerfold, permitting the binding to open almost flat, and strengthening the entire book block.

**Spine:** The back of a bound book connecting the two covers. Title, author's name, and sometimes publisher's imprint and/or ISBN are printed on it.

**Stripping:** Placing the various elements of the layout in their proper positions on the flats which will be used to make the final plates.

**Subsidy press:** A publishing company that applies its ISBN to a book and charges the author for the cost of production. The author receives only a few copies of the book, and is promised royalties on those copies that might be sold by the subsidy press.

## —T—

**Tag:** In HTML, the code that will tells browser software to apply, or to stop applying, a certain type of style or format to a part of a document.

**Title page:** The page in a book's front matter, usually recto, which states the title, author, and publisher. Follows half-title page.

**Trade paperback:** The name given to the common soft cover books sold in bookstores Usually they are 6- by- 9 or 5½- by- 8½ inches in size and are printed on substantial paper. Not "mass market."

**Trap**: An area of overlapping ink where different colors of ink meet. Traps prevent unwanted white edges, where the paper color shows through, between areas of different colors.

**Typeface:** A style or design of type encompassing shape, weight, and proportions which make it distinct from other typefaces. Use a conventional typeface for your body text.

**Typo:** Another word for typographical error. Find them during the proofing process, not at blueline stage or after the book is in print.

## —U —

**UV coating:** A liquid protective coating applied to covers or dust jackets during the printing process that is dried by means of ultraviolet lights. Not as protective as film lamination, but better than varnish.

**Uncoated** paper: Paper on which the printing surface consists of the paper stock itself. Usually used to print the body of the book. Books made with uncoated cover stock (card stock) usually look "homemade."

**Underlining:** Don't use it for titles or emphasis in books. Use *italics*.

**URL:** Universal Resource Locator. The "address" of a site on the World Wide Web.

## —V—

**Vanity press:** Another term for a subsidy press. It implies that the published book has no value other than to stroke the author's ego.

**Varnish:** A thin protective coating applied to a printed sheet or cover during the printing process. It provides protection and gloss for appearance; cheaper than lamination, but with less gloss and providing less protection.

**Verso:** A left-hand page of a book, properly an even-numbered page. *The* verso page contains the copyright and other important information.

## —W—

**Walk-around:** A person dressed in costume who walks around at a mall or shopping center during a booksigning to help promote a book.

**Web:** See World Wide Web.

**Webmaster:** A computer buff who is able to produce exceptionally striking art and format of pages on the World Wide Web.

**Web press:** A printing press that uses large rolls of paper rather than individual sheets. Economical for long print runs (more than 10,000 copies). Newspapers and magazines are printed on web presses.

**Web page:** A page on a Web site, usually the Home page, but any page if the site has more than one page.

**Wholesale:** A price given to re-sellers which reflects a discount from the stated retail price.

**Widow:** A short single line at the top of a page or column, usually the last line of the last paragraph from the preceding page; to be avoided in good typesetting. Also, a single word or syllable produced by a bad break standing alone as the last line of a paragraph.

**World Wide Web:** The network of personal and commercial information sites on the computer-served Internet. The World Wide Web is the host for individual Web sites which consist of Home pages and other pages connected to the Home pages via hyperlinks.

**—Z—**

**Zee:** secret for success is to do the book right.

# Index

## - Q -

## - R -

## - T -

# About the authors

LINDA AND JIM SALISBURY, award-winning publishers and book packagers, founded Tabby House in 1990 in order to publish Linda's second book. Her first book, *Good-bye Tomato, Hello Florida* (Phoenix Press), was on the Southwest Florida best-seller list for several months. Tabby House's first effort, *Read My Lips: No New Pets!*, brought an honorable mention in the National Association of Independent Publishers (NAIP) new book contest, and a steady stream of requests for help from other self-publishing authors. Their book packaging business has continued to grow in scope and stature ever since. Tabby House now selectively packages twelve to eighteen books every year.

Linda was graduated from Oberlin College with a B.A. in English. She is an editorial writer and columnist with a major Southwest Florida newspaper, and has had extensive experience in marketing and public relations.

Jim, a graduate of Upsala College with a B.S. in geology, spent many years teaching science at Pingry School in New Jersey. He has served as president of the Florida Publishers Association and remains on the Board of Directors.

In addition to providing book-packaging services to self-publishing authors, Jim and Linda present informative seminars on self-publishing to writer's groups and others interested in publishing their own books. This book is an outgrowth of the questions asked at those seminars, and their many varied experiences in the publishing industry.

Tabby House is a proud member of the National Association of Independent Publishers (NAIP), Publishers Association of the South (PAS), Southeast Booksellers Association (SEBA), Publishers Marketing Association (PMA), and the Florida Publishers Association (FPA).